Mortgage Smart
Know BEFORE You Buy

Rico Wilson, CFP®

Copyright © 2018 Rico Wilson

All rights reserved.

ISBN-10: 1985192101
ISBN-13: 978-1985192102

DEDICATION

To all of you aspiring homeowners out there. Nothing epitomizes the American Dream more than homeownership. Yes, it requires sacrifice and hard work, but over time it pays off. The lifestyle and pride of ownership you will experience will make it all worthwhile.

The financial rewards will also come to those with the patience and vision to stay the course and make it happen. Long term, individual homeownership has been highly instrumental in helping millions of Americans to achieve their goals.

Also – to all the Realtors and Loan Officers out there. Real Estate is a great business, but it is very challenging. It requires a lot of dedication to build a successful business in Real Estate & Real Estate Finance. "Cheers!" to your vision, hard work and commitment to excellence.

CONTENTS

	Acknowledgments	vii
1	Introduction: Why Read This Book?	1
2	The Home Buying Process	3
3	What is a Mortgage?	7
4	Amortization, Interest-Only, Balloon – Huh?	9
5	What is Negative Amortization?	15
6	What is a Pre-Payment Penalty?	17
7	Types of Mortgages	19
8	Fixed vs. Variable Rates	25
9	Mortgage Insurance (MI)	31
10	How Mortgages are Priced	35
11	Annual Percentage Rate (APR)	43
12	The Secondary Market	47
13	Choosing the Right Loan Product	51
14	Should You Pay Points?	55
15	Escrowing for Taxes & Insurance	61
16	Pro-Rated Interest	69
17	Loan-to-Value, Housing Ratio, Debt Ratio	71
18	Closing Costs	79

CONTENTS, CONT.

19	How to Choose a Lender	83
20	Get Your Documents Ready	91
21	The Loan Estimate (LE) and Closing Disclosure (CD)	97
22	Down Payment Assistance (DPA) Programs	99
23	Should You Refinance?	103
24	What is an Amortization Schedule?	109
25	Pre-Paying Principal to Reduce Interest Charges	131
26	What is a Recast?	137
27	Reverse Mortgages, HELOC's, Land Loans, Construction Loans, Renovation Loans, Subdivision Sales	141
28	Conclusion – What? Already?	153

ACKNOWLEDGMENTS

I got my first Real Estate license in 1983. My first boss at my first Real Estate company told me that the first thing I had to do was to learn Real Estate Finance. So, I found a mentor, bought a text book and took "real estate finance lessons".

Since then, I have also been a stock broker, a financial advisor, and have now been a Certified Financial Planner® for over 20 years. About 10 years ago, I developed an innovative real estate investment strategy and taught the procedure in my book of the same title, *The Rico Strategy*®.

After many years in both Real Estate and Finance, it only makes sense that I have found a career for myself in Mortgage Banking. And I think I have finally been doing this for long enough now to feel like I might be starting to get the hang of it.

I must acknowledge that, over the past 35 years, there have been a number of people (whose names will not be mentioned here because there are too many of them) who have helped me to learn about Real Estate, Finance and Mortgage Banking. To all these people, you have my sincerest gratitude.

1

INTRODUCTION: WHY READ THIS BOOK?

There is a lot to know about mortgages. The mortgage industry and mortgage products have become much more complicated than it probably seems like they ought to be.

If you are considering buying a home, particularly for the first time, there is a lot that you probably do not yet know. You can attempt to learn as you go, but that does not assure that you will make the most informed decisions – and it certainly does not assure that you will have the most positive, comfortable experience.

Most people are in the dark and, to a large extent, just have to trust that they have a competent and honest mortgage loan officer assisting them. Of course, we always hope that this is the case – but it is preferable to also understand some basic information about mortgages. The object of this book is not to train mortgage professionals, and I will do my best to make this book as un-technical as possible.

The purpose of this book is to explain what a borrower would benefit from knowing about before getting a mortgage. There are things in this book that may interest you greatly, and other things that may not interest you at all. Please feel free to use this source of information however you feel it will benefit you the most. I will not be offended if you look through it and only read the specific sections that you have an interest in.

Whether you are a first-time homebuyer or have already bought and sold numerous properties, if you feel like you would like to know more about mortgages before taking on this massive, long-term commitment, this book is for you.

2

THE HOME BUYING PROCESS

If you are new to the process of borrowing money to purchase real estate, a brief overview should be of interest to you. This section will address this topic at a very high level, so that you can see the big picture of how the process works. The details of your specific transaction may not exactly follow this outline, but they should at least resemble it.

1. You do some type of mortgage application – via phone, internet or in person.

2. A **_Loan Officer (LO)_** will review your credit report and the information you submitted in order to be able to issue you a written **_Pre-Approval Letter._** You may need to submit income and asset documentation at this time, especially if you are self-employed.

3. Your Realtor also gets a copy of this Pre-Approval Letter and will now be able to show you some available homes, and help you to select one that you would like to own.

4. You and your Realtor complete a written offer to purchase your chosen property. There may be a little negotiating at this time but, hopefully, this will result in an accepted offer/contract. You should be prepared to pay for the earnest deposit, option deposit, home inspection and appraisal at this time.

5. Your Realtor will help you to order a property inspection on the home. You have probably paid a small option deposit for the right to terminate the contract within 7 days or so. This is mainly to make sure that the property is in acceptable condition to you before you are locked into your purchase.

6. You and/or your Realtor will get a copy of your contract to your loan officer so that (s)he can start the loan process. You will receive a ***Loan Estimate (LE)*** and some disclosures to sign. You will also have the opportunity to lock your interest rate at this time.

7. You will be asked to pay for an appraisal on the property, probably using a credit card online. The appraisal will be ordered, but

should not be completed until you have had a chance to review the home inspector's findings regarding the home's condition.

If the condition is unsatisfactory and you decide to terminate the contract, you should receive a refund of your appraisal fee – as long as you cancel your loan before the appraiser has inspected the property.

(If you terminate the contract within the option period, you should also receive a refund of your earnest deposit.)

8. Your lender's ***Mortgage Processor*** will be "processing" your loan at this time. They will need you to provide a list of documents so that they can do a complete evaluation of all important factors before your loan gets final approval. This may require that you provide additional documentation during the process.

9. Once your Processor has completed all their tasks, your file is ready to be forwarded to a ***Mortgage Underwriter.*** Your Underwriter will review all the information in the file before issuing a ***Final Approval.*** You will likely get a ***Conditional Approval*** before the Final Approval. This just means that your loan is approved, subject to the Underwriter receiving something – probably some other

document(s) that you will need to provide.

10. Your file will then be assigned a ***Closer***. You will receive a ***Closing Disclosure (CD)***, which will go over all the final numbers of the transaction. You will have an appointment set up with the ***Title Company*** (or attorney, in some states) to sign the final papers ("closing doc's") and exchange money.

11. You will probably wire your **cash-to-close** (the remainder of your down payment and closing costs) to the title company the night before closing. The lender will also wire to the title company the proceeds of your mortgage loan.

12. On closing day, after all the closing documents have been signed by all buyers and sellers, the title company will distribute the funds due to the seller(s), and you will now be the proud owner of your new home. You will receive a copy of the final closing doc's, and begin making monthly mortgage payments to repay the money that you borrowed to purchase the home.

Again, this is just a brief overview of the process and transactions vary. This overview should at least resemble the process that you will go through when you purchase your home.

3

WHAT IS A MORTGAGE?

The term ***mortgage*** refers to the type of loan that is used to buy or refinance a piece of real property, or real estate. This term is most commonly used to mean a loan to purchase or refinance a home (house, condo, etc.).

The home becomes collateral, or security for the loan, so that if you default on the loan legal ownership of the home can be taken away from you through a legal process called ***foreclosure***. (Real estate is not repossessed, it is foreclosed upon.) Once the loan is paid in full, the home is no longer ***hypothecated***, or used as security for the loan and you should receive a ***release of lien***, which should also be filed at the county records office in the county where the property is located.

To obtain a mortgage, you would work with a

Mortgage Loan Originator (loan officer, loan consultant, mortgage banker, mortgage broker, etc.). You would find this person at a bank, credit union, mortgage company or mortgage brokerage office.

The person who assists the loan officer with putting a complete file together to submit for loan approval is usually called a ***processor***, and the person who actually approves or denies the loan is called an ***underwriter***.

Some states, referred to as ***trust deed states***, use a ***note*** and ***deed of trust*** instead of a mortgage. This is a different set of documents that serves the same overall purpose.

If you are in a trust deed state, you will sign a note, which is a promise to repay the debt, and the deed to the home will be "held in trust" with a designated ***trustee*** until the loan is paid in full. These alternative legal instruments, and the process in general, will still be referred to using the term "mortgage" and the players will still be "mortgage" professionals in the "mortgage" business.

4

AMORTIZATION, INTEREST-ONLY, BALLOON – HUH?

A mortgage can be *interest-only* or *amortized*. An amortized loan can be *fully-amortized* or can require a *balloon payment*.

An **interest-only loan** allows you to pay only the interest **accrued** (interest that has accumulated to that point in time) every month without paying anything toward principal (the loan balance). The principal balance will not be reduced as long as no principal payments are being made, so the amount you owe will stay the same while you are only making interest-only payments.

The interest-only option is generally a temporary provision that allows a borrower to make a lower monthly payment than would be due with a regular, amortized loan, for a finite period of time such as 10 years.

With many interest-only loans, after the initial 10-year period, the loan would automatically become a fully-amortized loan for a period of 20 years. So, the entire loan period would be 30 years but the first 10 years would offer a reduced payment due to the interest-only provision.

Note that after the initial 10-year period, the monthly payment would actually go up to an amount higher than a normal 30-year amortized loan because the entire principal balance would now have to be paid back over 20 years, not 30 years.

There are a variety of reasons why someone would be interested in an interest-only loan. It could be that you need a lower payment to be comfortable with the home you wish to purchase, and you anticipate your income going up substantially during the interest-only period, so that when the amortization period starts, increasing your monthly payment, you will be prepared for that higher payment.

Hopefully, you also have good reason to believe that there will be significant appreciation in your local real estate market during that time so that you are also building equity in the home even though you are not reducing the loan amount during that time.

Many people utilizing an interest-only option do so

believing that the home will appreciate in value significantly during that time, and that before the interest-only period is up they will either sell the home or refinance the mortgage.

Whatever the reason might be, it is a good idea to have some definite reason for choosing this option – and if there isn't a good reason, a fully-amortized loan is probably a better long-term strategy.

Interest rates will probably be slightly higher with an interest-only loan as well, so for this option to be the right one, lower monthly payments should probably be significantly more important to you than reducing the loan balance during the interest-only period.

Another reason to use an interest-only mortgage would be if you are in a situation where your income is sporadic but substantial. If you need to minimize your monthly obligations, but you have the ability to make large principal-reduction payments every 6-12 months or so, an interest-only option might be a good idea.

Some people have the means to comfortably pay off their entire mortgage within a 10-year period, but cannot commit to a large payment every single month. Even if the mortgage is not entirely paid off within the initial interest-only period, if it is substantially reduced within that period, it might have been a good idea.

For example, let's say that a commercial real estate agent who earns $500,000 to $1,000,000 per year, but only gets paid once or twice a year, wants a mortgage of $900,000. An interest-only payment might be quite a bit lower than a fully-amortized payment. If the interest-only period is 10 years, and within that time he/she pays down the mortgage to $200,000, that creates a relatively small payment when the loan converts to a fully-amortized, 20-year fixed loan at the end of the interest-only period.

An ***amortized loan*** simply means that, through a complex calculation that is always best left to a computer or financial calculator, a monthly payment amount is calculated that will result in all interest and principal due being paid in full at the end of the ***amortization period***. The monthly payment stays the same (if you chose a fixed rate), but the amount of each payment that goes to principal versus interest changes monthly.

For example, if you have a $250,000 loan at 4.5% interest for 30 years, your principal and interest payment would be $1,266.71/month. That payment will not change – but how that payment is divided between principal and interest will change.

At the end of the first month, you will have accrued an interest charge of $937.50. (4.5% / 12 months x $250,000). After that interest charge is deducted from your first monthly payment, there will be $329.21 left over that will be put toward reducing your principal balance.

Because your principal balance has been reduced after your first payment, the interest charged in the second month will be slightly less at $936.27 (4.5% / 12 months x $249, 670.79). That leaves $1.23 more from your second monthly payment to go toward reducing your principal balance.

Over time, more and more of that same monthly payment is going toward principal because the actual interest charge for that month is reduced from what it was the month before, due to your declining principal balance. When it comes time to make your final payment, that payment is almost entirely principal because the interest charge is so low when your loan is almost paid off.

What I just described would be called a ***fully-amortized loan***, because you make a series of payments (equal payments, if you have a fixed rate) and when those payments have all been made, your loan is paid in full.

Instead of a fully-amortized loan, you could also have an amortized loan with a ***balloon payment***. This means that you would still have an amortized loan with an amortization period of, let's say, 30 years like the example above. But, instead of taking the full 30 years to pay off the loan, after 5 or 10 years, or at some other point in time, you would be required to pay in full whatever principal balance is still owed at that time.

In this case, you have been making payments for some period of time and a part of that monthly payment has been going toward principal reduction. So, when the balloon payment is due you do not have to pay the entire principal amount you borrowed – some part of that has already been paid through your monthly mortgage payment. You would only have to pay the amount that is still owed at that time.

You could do this from your savings account, by selling the home, or by refinancing the home – taking out a new mortgage to pay off the existing mortgage. In any case, when the balloon payment is due, you have to have a plan as to how you are going to make that large payment.

Balloon payments do not seem to be in use with traditional mortgage financing at the moment – these are more commonly associated with ***alternative financing*** such as seller financing, that is designed to be temporary financing until more traditional financing can be obtained. If you are applying for a conventional or government-backed mortgage, you probably do not need to worry about a balloon payment – but it's good to know that the term means.

5

WHAT IS NEGATIVE AMORTIZATION?

We talked about interest-only financing – making a monthly payment that only covers the interest accrued on the loan, with nothing left to reduce your principal balance. Well, what do you think would happen if a loan only required a monthly payment that was so low that it did not even pay all of the interest that had accrued during that month?

This is a ***negative-amortization*** loan. The monthly payment is a lower amount than the interest accrued, so that every month the amount of interest that was not paid has to be added to the principal balance of the loan.

So, every month you make your mortgage payment – only, instead of your loan balance going down a little each month – it goes up! And when interest owed is added to your principal balance, the interest charges increase. Now, you're paying interest on top of interest!

Yeah, that sounds like a great idea, doesn't it? (Yes, I am being sarcastic.) Are there any possible risks that come to mind with this type of a loan? Well, believe it or not, there were some legitimate uses for this type of loan – but the risk of default is much higher.

This is simply not a suitable loan for most people in most situations. These loans resulted in a large percentage of foreclosures in the past and do not seem to be in use at all in what we would call ***traditional financing*** at the moment.

Again, this is something you really won't need to worry about, but many people still want to know what it is. Now you know.

6

WHAT IS A PRE-PAYMENT PENALTY?

Mortgage lending is a business and, like any business, it needs to be profitable. There are a variety of ways that mortgage lenders can earn a profit, and if a particular type of loan requires that a certain number of payments be made for the lender to avoid losing money on that loan, sometimes a *pre-payment penalty* is used to try to prevent that loss from happening.

A **pre-payment penalty** is some amount that must be paid to the lender in excess of the actual principal and interest due at the time, if the loan is being paid off (or significantly paid down) before some required minimum amount of time has passed.

This is usually a relatively small amount and decreases gradually to zero over the first three years or so. This is simply to make sure that the lender locks in some minimal profit, or at least doesn't lose money if a borrower refinances too soon. It is not necessarily an evil or abusive thing, but it is definitely something you need to understand before committing to a mortgage that includes this provision.

Fortunately, you won't find pre-payment penalties with traditional financing anymore – at least not any loans that I have. This provision is usually used with certain alternative, non-conforming financing options and should not necessarily dissuade a suitable borrower from utilizing that loan – it just needs to be understood upfront.

7

TYPES OF MORTGAGES

There are many types of mortgages. The one you should choose will usually come down to which "box" you fit into best. The requirements vary widely enough that, very often, it is easy to decide which option to pursue.

If you qualify, a ***conventional loan*** will usually be the preferred option. These generally have the best set of terms, overall. If your loan amount does not exceed $453,100 (the new limit as of 2018), your conventional loan is referred to as a ***conforming*** loan.

This means that the loan conforms to ***Fannie Mae*** (Federal National Mortgage Association, FNMA) or ***Freddie Mac*** (Federal Home Loan Mortgage Corporation, FHLMC) guidelines so that the loan can be sold to one of these ***Government Sponsored***

Enterprises (GSEs) once it has closed.

A couple of notes regarding the above paragraph:

1. If the idea of selling loans after closing is new to you, we'll cover the secondary market in another section and it will make perfect sense.

2. The $453,100 limit is for single-unit properties and does not include ***high-cost areas*** which have higher limits.

If your loan amount is above $453,100 (excluding areas that are designated "high-cost"), you will need a ***non-conforming, "jumbo"*** loan. These loans are for loan amounts that exceed the conforming loan limit. The qualifying guidelines are a little stricter and rates are usually a little bit higher.

If the conventional loan "box" is not the right fit for you for some reason or another, you may consider a ***government loan***. This usually means FHA or VA. If you are not a qualifying veteran, this probably means FHA.

A ***FHA loan*** is a loan that is insured by the federal government through the ***Federal Housing Administration***. The FHA was created to help more people to be able to own their own homes. In most cases, it is easier to qualify for a FHA loan than it is for a conventional loan.

FHA loan guidelines are generally more lenient than conventional loan guidelines are when it comes to your down payment and your credit score. Depending on the borrower, the interest rate may also be a little lower on a FHA loan than on a conventional.

It is good to be aware, however, that even if the conventional loan requires mortgage insurance, the FHA mortgage insurance is probably more expensive and there is no option to avoid it with FHA like there is with a conventional loan. (I will cover mortgage insurance very shortly.)

FHA loans are the most popular choice for first-time homebuyers due to the lower minimum down payment, lower minimum credit score, more flexibility regarding the credit report, and a higher percentage of gross monthly income that can be used to qualify.

It is also important to know that the loan limit is lower than with conventional loans. This limit varies by area with the minimum limit at $294,515. The limit in my area (Austin, Texas) is presently $384,100. In the most expensive real estate markets in the country, the limit is $636,150.

If you qualify for a **VA loan** through the **Veteran's Administration**, you may qualify for a zero down payment loan.

VA loans require a **VA Funding Fee** instead of mortgage insurance, which enables the VA to guarantee a portion of the loan so that the zero down payment option is possible. The VA funding fee can be partially or fully waived if the borrower is a qualifying disabled veteran.

The loan limit for VA loans with zero down payment is generally the same the conforming conventional loan limit, which is presently $453,100.

If you are considering a VA loan, remember that even though you may not have to make a down payment, you will probably have to pay for at least some of the closing costs.

In addition to conventional and government loan programs, a mortgage can also be ***portfolio*** loan. This is a type of non-conforming loan that is generally not designed to be sold to the *conduits* in the secondary market in order to be packaged, securitized and resold to investors. (Don't worry, I will explain this a little later.)

A portfolio loan may still be subject to **ATR regulations** (making sure that the borrower has the "Ability To Repay" the loan before offering it), but can be much more flexible regarding other qualifying requirements.

For example, with conventional and government

loans, a Chapter 7 Bankruptcy must be discharged for a certain number of years before a borrower is eligible to obtain financing. I presently have a "portfolio product" that will allow a borrower to start the mortgage process one day after a Chapter 7 discharge, as long as their credit score is at least 580 and their debt-to-income ratio does not exceed 50%.

Of course, there are other details you would need to be aware of, and the interest rate will be higher than a conventional or government loan. But this could be a great solution for the right borrower.

8

FIXED VS. VARIABLE RATES

You can choose a mortgage loan with a ***fixed rate*** or a ***variable rate***. A fixed rate, such as a 30-year fixed, will have the same interest rate for the entire duration of the loan term. Right now, the 30-year fixed is the most popular type of loan. This is often a good choice when interest rates are low and unlikely to go much lower.

A variable rate, such as those offered with an ***adjustable rate mortgage (ARM)***, can also be an attractive choice depending upon the circumstances.

For example, a 7/1 ARM is a mortgage that will usually start out with a little lower interest rate than a 30-year fixed, but that rate will only be locked in for 7 years. After that time, the rate will start to adjust, and may adjust annually if rates move during that year.

In addition, the starting rate may be a little lower than it would normally be (sometimes referred to as a *teaser rate*), so that even if market rates do not go up, your rate may very well go up at the end of the initial 7-year period.

A 5/1 ARM is like a 7/1 ARM but the initial fixed period is locked for 5 years instead of 7. (The "1" means that after the initial locked period, your interest rate can adjust as often as every "1" year.) Because of the shorter fixed period, initial 5/1 ARM rates are usually a little lower than 7/1 ARM initial rates.

If you are tempted by the lower initial rates associated with ARM's compared to a fixed rate, make sure you think it through first. It may be your best choice – but have a reason before making that choice.

Maybe the kids will have all left the next in the next 7 years and you will want to sell your two-story home and down-size to a smaller, single-level. If you are pretty sure that is what you want to do, then maybe a 7/1 ARM would be a good choice because it will save you some interest expense.

If you're not going to have the loan at the time the rate would make its initial adjustment, then the lower rate for the first few years may be something you should take advantage of.

But what happens if you decide to stay in that home

for a long time and market interest rates are significantly higher when rate-adjustment time comes?

If you stay in the home (and still need a mortgage), you'll either have to refinance at now higher rates or suffer periodic rate changes at the whim of the market.

If there is any realistic chance that you will need or want to keep the mortgage for longer than the fixed-rate period, you will want to be familiar with rate caps.

Rate caps determine how much your rate can adjust at certain times during the life of your mortgage. There are three different rate caps you should be aware of:

1. Initial Adjustment Cap

2. Subsequent Adjustment Cap

3. Lifetime Adjustment Cap

The types of adjustable rate loans we have been talking about are called ***Hybrid ARM's*** because they start with a fixed-rate period and then become adjustable rate mortgages. Hybrid ARM's give you the advantage of a low fixed rate for some period of time – but if you keep the loan beyond that time, be prepared for a spanking.

After you have taken advantage of a Hybrid ARM's

generosity for the fixed-rate period, the initial interest rate jump afterwards can be shocking. Subsequent adjustments are probably more moderate, though still significant. And, finally, the lifetime adjustment cap makes sure that there is some limit on how much your rate can change over the life of your loan.

For example, let's say that you have the following type of loan:

5/1 ARM with 5/2/5 Caps

First of all, you can tell this is a hybrid because the 5/1 means that your initial rate is fixed for 5 years, then your rate can adjust as often as every "1" year.

Next, you can see that your caps will be:

- ***Initial Adjustment Cap*** – limited to an interest rate increase of 5%. (Also limited to an interest rate decrease of 5%, but good luck needing that limit.)

- ***Subsequent Adjustment Cap*** – limited to an interest rate increase (or decrease) of 2% per year. This can adjust as often as every year because of the "1" in 5/1 ARM.

- ***Lifetime Adjustment Cap*** of 5%, which you could be hit with all at once in the initial adjustment if interest rates have gone up very much since you got your mortgage.

Be aware that interest rates do not have to go up by 5% for you to be hit with a 5% increase in your first rate adjustment. Your starter rate (teaser rate) may be lower than what the fully indexed rate actually was when you got your mortgage.

The ***fully-indexed rate*** is the current rate of the ***index*** they are using, plus the ***margin*** that they add to that index. The most commonly used index is the ***LIBOR***, or ***London Inter-Bank Offered Rate***. The margin will probably be around 2.25%, which is added to the LIBOR rate to determine the fully-indexed rate.

For example, if the LIBOR rate is 2.5% and the margin is 2.25%, your fully-indexed rate is 4.75%. If your 5/1 ARM starter rate is only 3.75%, interest rates will not have to move at all for you to be hit with a 1% increase at your initial adjustment. If rates are low now and they go up 1-2% over the next 5 years, the initial rate adjustment may not be very comfortable for you.

Many times, a borrower will use an ARM to make it easier to qualify for the loan they want. A lower monthly payment results in a lower *housing ratio*. (Yes, I will cover this later.)

Be advised, however, that if you are using a hybrid ARM with a fixed rate period of less than 7 years, such as the 5/1 ARM in our example, you will probably be required to qualify at the fully indexed rate.

This means that they will use the higher payment that you would have, if your interest rate were the fully indexed rate, to calculate your housing and debt ratios (yes, I will explain these soon). If this is your reason for using an ARM, you will probably want to look at a 7/1 ARM, not a 3/1 or 5/1 ARM.

Generally speaking, if you're going to be in the house for a long time (and intend to keep a mortgage on the house for a long time) and interest rates are low, then a fixed-rate mortgage is probably a better way to go. If you're pretty positive that you will not be needing that mortgage for longer than the initial locked-in period, then consider an ARM.

Again, an adjustable rate mortgage may be a good choice for you, but make sure to think it through first. This book does not attempt to go every detail regarding adjustable rate mortgages. If you are considering an ARM, I suggest working with a competent loan officer for current information on your best ARM options.

9

MORTGAGE INSURANCE (MI)

In the context of mortgage financing, ***mortgage insurance (MI)*** should not be confused with a life insurance policy that correlates with your declining mortgage balance and is designed specifically to pay off your home if you die, so that surviving family members aren't burdened with that debt. That life insurance product is also often referred to as "mortgage insurance", but that is not what we are referring to here.

Until recent years, a person had to pay a 20% down payment in order to get a ***purchase money mortgage*** (a mortgage for the purpose of buying a home, rather than refinancing). That excluded many people who wanted to buy a home because they were not able to come up with that large chunk of money. They could try to save it over time, but home prices were increasing while they were trying to save.

Finally, somebody came up with a brilliant idea. The reason why lenders required 20% down was to mitigate their risk of defaulted loans, and the risk of losing money when they had to foreclose on a property. 20% down makes it less likely that a buyer will default, and also reduces the financial loss to the lender when a foreclosure is necessary.

Is there something else that could mitigate that risk? Why, yes there is, thank you for asking. It's called *insurance*. All kinds of risks are transferred to insurance companies through the purchase of some kind of insurance policy – why not design an insurance product for this? So, they did.

And this insurance does not have to cover the entire value of the property – selling the foreclosed property will reimburse a large percentage of the potential loss. But they need to cover part of the potential loss through either a large down payment, an insurance policy, or a fund that acts as self-insurance by imposing on each loan a fee that is placed into that fund.

All three of these methods are presently in use. If a homebuyer does not have 20% to put down, they can put as little as 5% down on a conforming conventional loan and pay for **private mortgage insurance (PMI)**. (There are a couple of programs right now that only require 3% down; however, there are restrictions.)

Or, they can put as little as 3.5% down on a FHA loan and pay a *mortgage insurance premium (MIP)*. Or, if they get a VA loan or a USDA loan (for qualifying rural areas), they would pay a *funding fee* instead of mortgage insurance.

Some other specialized mortgage products use an increased interest rate to fund the pool to mitigate the lender's risk of loss.

Lender-paid mortgage insurance (LPMI) is one example of mortgage insurance being built into the interest rate. With conventional loans, you may have the option of accepting a higher interest rate instead of adding a monthly PMI payment to your loan. In exchange for accepting a higher rate, the lender will pay for your mortgage insurance.

The advantage to this would be that your monthly payment will probably be lower, possibly helping you to qualify from a *debt-to-income ratio* standpoint. The disadvantage would be that the interest rate you choose is for the life of the loan, whereas borrower-paid PMI can be removed when your *loan-to-value* drops to under 80%. (We will go over ratios soon...)

A conforming conventional loan generally charges less for mortgage insurance than a FHA loan does. The monthly payment may be similar but, in addition to the monthly premium, FHA loans also impose an *upfront MIP* amount (usually 1.75% of the loan amount) that is generally added to the loan amount so that interest is also being paid on that portion of the total MIP.

New FHA loans all require MIP and it is not removed when you have more equity in the home (unless your down payment was at least 10%, and then you still have to wait 11 years).

Conventional loans have a variety of options to cancel PMI. At the very least, you will have to have 20% equity in your home, wait for at least 2 years, and it may require a new appraisal. In some situations, the PMI can drop off automatically. There are different requirements for different situations.

It is important to understand that mortgage insurance is not an evil rip-off. It enables people who cannot put 20% down to purchase a home. However, the bottom line is that you are paying for something that does not benefit you beyond that – mortgage insurance protects the lender, not you. So, I would avoid it if is practical to do so.

If you are able to put 20% down, that is generally a good idea. If not, paying mortgage insurance is not the end of the world and is probably preferable to renting if you really want to own your own home.

10

HOW MORTGAGES ARE PRICED

This area is a complete mystery to most borrowers, but one that could be very useful to understand. Here is an example of a typical mortgage pricing grid for a $250,000 conventional 30-year fixed loan:

Interest Rate	Cost/Credit %	Cost/Credit $	P & I Payment
4.000%	3.062%	($7,655.00)	$1,194.00
4.125%	2.385%	($5,962.50)	$1,212.00
4.250%	1.834%	($4,585.00)	$1,230.00
4.375%	1.335%	($3,337.50)	$1,248.00
4.500%	0.765%	($1,912.50)	$1,267.00
4.625%	0.270%	($675.00)	$1,285.00
4.750%	(0.166%)	$415.00	$1,304.00
4.875%	(0.594%)	$1,485.00	$1,323.00
5.000%	(0.978%)	$2,445.00	$1,342.00
5.125%	(1.415%)	$3,537.50	$1,361.00

I should interject here that this is one, specific scenario. Rates, or more accurately, "pricing", can vary depending upon a number of factors including loan program, type of property, amount of down payment, credit score, length of rate lock, whether you have an escrow account, etc. And the rate you select will **float** until you **lock** it.

The first thing you might notice from the pricing grid above is that there is not just one, single interest rate – there are a variety of rates to choose from, depending on all that other stuff in those other boxes. Let's go through this now.

The first column (far left) shows a variety of interest rates that would be available in this specific situation. The second column (from the left) shows how much you would have to pay for one of the lower rates, or how much you would receive for accepting one of the higher rates, listed to the left of that cost or credit percentage.

The parentheses indicate that this value is a credit to you, usually an amount that will be subtracted from your closing costs, reducing your total **cash-to-close** – the total amount you will need to bring to closing.

You may hear the terms *points* and *basis points*. A **point** is 1% of your loan amount. A **basis point** is 1/100 of a point. This is often abbreviated **bps** for the plural, basis points, and pronounced "**bips**".

So, looking at the grid above, if you want an interest rate of 4.625%, it will cost you 27 bps (0.270%). If you are willing to accept a little higher interest rate, let's say 4.875%, you will receive a credit toward your closing cost of almost 60 bps (0.594%).

The practice of paying this percentage in order to obtain a lower interest rate is called ***paying points*** or ***buying down the rate***. If you would prefer a credit toward your closing costs, I can ***premium-price*** your loan, which means that I will offer you a higher interest rate in exchange for the credit that correlates to that interest rate in your pricing grid.

The terms "point" and "percent" should not necessarily be considered to be interchangeable as "percent" is used more often regarding the down payment amount, so this would be a percentage of the purchase price of the home, not a percentage of the loan amount.

A "point" is more appropriately used as a percentage of the loan amount, not the purchase price. Keeping those terms separate in this way can help to avoid confusion regarding what number is being used when calculating points or down payment.

Just to make this very clear, if you put 10 percent (10%) down on the purchase of a $300,000 home, your down payment is $30,000 (10% of the $300,000 purchase price). If you then pay 1 point (1%) to buy down the interest rate, you are paying $2,700, not $3,000, because that 1 point is 1% of the loan amount ($270,000), not 1% of the purchase price.

The third column (from the left) is simply the dollar amount that results when you multiply the interest rate in the first column by the percentage in the second column (in the same row, of course). In this column, the parentheses indicate that this is a cost to you. No parentheses indicates that this amount is a credit to you.

For example, if you wanted to receive a credit toward your closing costs and you were perfectly happy with an interest rate of 5.0%, you would receive a credit of almost 1 point (97.8 bps), which multiplied by the loan amount (not purchase price) equals $2,445.

The last column (far right) shows the amount of your ***P & I Payment***. This means just the amount required to repay the mortgage debt – this does not include property taxes, homeowner's insurance, and mortgage insurance (MI) or homeowner's association/condo dues.

If you have an escrow account, your actual monthly payment will be higher than this, so that you are paying a part of your annual tax and insurance bill every month when you make your mortgage payment. That payment may be referred to as a ***PITI*** payment, which covers Principal, Interest, Taxes and Insurance.

If you also have mortgage insurance (MI), you might see something like ***PITI+MI*** to include the MI in your payment as well. (Homeowner's Association or condo dues is generally paid separately from your mortgage payment, though it is included in your "housing ratio". We will talk about ratios shortly.)

By looking at the grid above, you can see what impact the interest rate you choose will have on your monthly mortgage payment. Then you can prioritize whether you would rather have a nice credit toward your closing costs, or if you would prefer to have a slightly lower payment for as long as you keep your loan. You can even calculate a *break-even time* to help you decide.

For example, using the grid above, if you are comparing a 4.0% interest rate to a 4.5% rate, you will see that the 4.0% rate will cost you 3.062 points, or just over 306 bps, where the 4.5% rate will cost you only 76.5 bps.

For the $250,000 loan amount in the example, that translates to a cash difference out of your pocket of $7,655 - $1,912.50 = $5,742.50. The monthly amount you would save by buying down the rate would be $1,267 - $1,194 = $73. That means that you would be paying $5,742.50 up front in order to save $73 on an ongoing basis.

Dividing the upfront payment by the monthly savings

shows that it will take 78.66 months to recover your $5,742.50 by saving $73 per month. That's just over 6 ½ years to get your money back. In most cases, I would not recommend choosing the lower interest rate at this price.

Here's an example that you might be more likely to come across. Let's say that you like the 4.625% interest rate and it only costs 27 bps. But, you really need to reduce your closing costs so that you have money to pay for moving expenses, etc.

If you choose the 5.0% rate instead, instead of paying $675 you would get back $2,445. That a difference of $3,120 that you can use for other expenses. Your payment will go up $57 per month, but if the cash-to-close is more important than the difference in monthly payment, that might be a good choice for you.

You may notice, looking at the grid, that there is no interest rate listed at zero points/zero credit. Sometimes there is, sometimes there is not. If there were, that would be considered a ***par rate***.

In many cases, a rate close to par would be a good choice because you are not taking an extra high rate that will cause your payment to be higher than necessary – and you're not paying a large chunk of money to pre-pay interest when the break-even period may be rather long.

When you talk to your loan officer about interest rates, you might ask about the par rate, paying points or receiving a credit before you decide which rate you want. Remember that there is not just one interest rate – you can choose which rate you want based on the cost or credit associated with that rate.

11

ANNUAL PERCENTAGE RATE (APR)

I get a lot of questions about APR. The same questions, actually, but I get them pretty often. One of the most common questions I get is whether it is the APR that determines your monthly payment or the interest rate. Let me explain APR – this will make you feel smart when you go shopping for a mortgage.

APR stands for **_Annual Percentage Rate_**. This is *not* your interest rate – and this is *not* the rate that determines your monthly P&I payment (the principal and interest portion of your entire monthly payment).

The Annual Percentage Rate tells you your actual yearly cost of borrowing that mortgage amount over the loan period – but as a percentage, not a dollar amount. It includes your interest rate plus other fees connected with borrowing that money, such as any loan origination fees or points paid to buy down the rate.

The APR does not include *all* of your closing costs because some of those closing costs are not due to the loan itself. Some of those costs are going to apply whether you use a mortgage or pay cash to purchase the home. For example, homeowner's insurance, title insurance and recording fees. Those are costs of purchasing a home, but they are not due to obtaining a mortgage to purchase the home.

How is APR useful? When you are shopping for a mortgage, you can compare interest rates and you can compare closing costs between lenders. But what if one lender's interest rate is lower than another, but its closing costs are substantially higher?

It is possible that the lender with the lower interest rate is buying down the rate – and increasing your closing costs to pay for that buydown. It might also be that the lender with the higher rate is premium-pricing the loan – offering you a higher interest rate in order to reduce your closing cost amount.

Using the APR can assist you in comparing the actual cost of financing between lenders. It can also help you to compare different types of loans. Let's look at a couple of examples:

First, let's say that Lender A offers you an interest

rate that is 0.25% lower than Lender B. But Lender A is also charging significantly higher closing costs than Lender B.

Being a mortgage banker, I would compare line items on the *Loan Estimate* to see what the specific differences are. But let's say that you don't want to go to that much trouble. You can compare the APR between the two lenders to give you a good idea of which one is really charging less overall.

Second, let's say that you are looking at a conventional loan versus a FHA loan. The FHA loan has a lower interest rate but the APR is higher than the conventional loan's APR. Why would this happen with the same lender on both loans?

Well, the mortgage insurance could be more expensive with the FHA loan than with the conventional – that is very common. The easiest way to see which loan will actually cost you less in the long run is to look at the APR's of both loans.

When deciding on a mortgage, APR is certainly not the only factor to consider. But, it is useful to be able to see what your actual cost of financing will be – including the interest rate and other charges.

12

THE SECONDARY MARKET

This is going to be a very non-technical explanation of how mortgages utilize a *secondary market* (you're welcome). All you need, and probably all you want, is a brief and easy-to-understand overview so that you'll know what's going on, and so that you'll understand what mortgage professionals are talking about if this subject comes up.

Investments that are referred to as *securities* are generally grouped into one of two categories: *equity* or *debt*. *"Equities"* usually refers to stocks – fractional ownership of a corporation.

"Debt Instruments" most often refers to bonds – IOU's issued by corporations or governments as a promise to repay borrowed money with interest. (The U.S. Treasury issues T-bills, T-bonds and T-notes. All of these are debt instruments.)

A mortgage note is also a promise to repay a debt with interest – kind of like a bond. When you borrow money to purchase a home, you have issued a long-term debt instrument.

Of course, this debt is very small when compared to a corporate or government bond issue. But mortgages can be grouped together, based on similar features such as the credit-worthiness of the borrower, to form a large debt instrument.

Just like governments or corporations, mortgage companies need to continuously raise money to keep operations going and make a profit. In other words, they need money to lend on an ongoing basis.

So, qualifying mortgages are sold to one of the ***conduits***, which then groups these mortgages together in packages called ***pools*** based on certain similar characteristics. These pools of mortgages are ***securitized***, or turned into securities – investments which are then are available to be purchased by large investors such as pension funds and insurance companies.

This is the reason why mortgage funds are now available to any "credit-worthy" borrower – and why mortgage interest rates are reasonable. Due to this secondary market, there is no shortage of money to lend because as soon as a lender lends to a borrower, that debt is sold (hopefully, at a profit), thereby replenishing the lenders funds so that the lender can then lend those funds to someone else.

13

CHOOSING THE RIGHT LOAN PRODUCT

Choosing the right loan product will very often come down to which "box" you fit into the best. Of course, you want to obtain the best terms that are available to you, so there is an order of priority to look at. That order probably goes something like this:

1) Conventional (conforming or jumbo, depending on loan amount)

2) Government (FHA, VA, etc.)

3) Alternative/Portfolio.

For example, a borrower with a 780 credit score, a great W2 job and lots of money in the bank should probably not go straight toward a FHA loan. Why not?

Because this borrower likely qualifies for a conventional loan that would not require MI (mortgage insurance). The APR will probably be lower on the conventional loan, even if the interest rate is slightly higher.

A borrower who intends to live in their new home for many years and is comfortable with the monthly payment amount of a fully-amortized, fixed-rate loan, when rates are close to historic lows (like right now), might want to lean more toward that loan instead of an interest-only (IO) or adjustable rate mortgage (ARM).

A borrower that doesn't seem to fit into any traditional box may need to resort to alternative financing such as a portfolio product or even seller-financing.

These options may carry higher interest rates, require a larger down payment and/or include a balloon payment due at some point, but this may still be preferable to not being able to obtain financing at all. Obviously, if you qualify for a top shelf, low interest loan, you probably won't even look at these other options.

The *term* of your loan is another thing you may want to think about. A 30-year term is the most common, but other terms are available. Personally, I like the interest rate break you get with a 15-year mortgage.

A 15-year mortgage requires a significantly larger monthly payment than a 30-year mortgage does. But, if you are planning on paying off the home early anyway, and you are comfortable with the higher monthly payment, you will be rewarded by a significant discount in interest rate compared to a 30-year loan.

With a 15-year loan, not only are you saving a lot of money in interest charges over the life of the loan, but you are also paying down principal at a much faster rate. People sometimes forget the benefits of simply not owing so much money.

If you owe $200,000, then you are able to pay off that debt quickly – you no longer owe $200,000! That's a lot of money you no longer have to come up with to repay a debt. That means that if you come up with that money anyway, you can use it for other things – you might even have more fun!

Many financial advisors would suggest sticking with a 30-year mortgage and investing the difference between the two payment choices in something that may offer you a greater **return on investment (ROI)**.

I believe that this must be judged on a case by case basis, so I cannot make any specific recommendation here. If you are interested in a mortgage with a term shorter than 30 years, you should consult with your loan officer and your financial advisor and decide for yourself what makes the most sense in your case.

When choosing a mortgage product, there may be a number of possible considerations depending upon the specifics of your situation. So, it is best to speak with an honest and competent loan originator to discuss what your options are.

As long as it is something that you qualify for, the decision is yours. But the loan officer can be very helpful in giving you the information you need to make the best decision for your individual situation.

14

SHOULD YOU PAY POINTS?

No. Next topic, please. Just kidding – well, kind of.

There are certain situations where it may make sense to pay points, and I have absolutely no problem with someone paying a few bps if there is no par rate and they would rather pay a little for a lower rate than get a small credit to take a higher rate. But, in general, I am not one to suggest paying points – at least not any significant amount in points. I would like to give you two examples to illustrate my rationale.

Example #1. I went into the real estate business in late 1983. I spent several years in the Scottsdale, Arizona area in subdivision sales, working for builder/developers. To the best of my recollection, during the four-year period from 1984 through 1987, I watched interest rates gradually go down from almost 14% to around 8%.

But another interesting thing was happening at the same time. Because rates were so high, builders wanted to offer below-market rates as an inducement to buy their homes. They paid points – a lot of points – to buy down those interest rates.

As an example, and this is approximate as I am just going off my memory here, let's say that the prevailing interest rate was 13%. A builder might offer a ***3-2-1 buydown*** that levels off at 11%. That means a homebuyer could buy a home with minimal down payment and make a monthly mortgage payment based on an interest rate of 8% during the first year (3% lower than the 11% where rate will stabilize).

In the second year, the monthly payment would be higher, as the applicable interest rate would be 9% (2% reduction from the 11% permanent rate). The third year, the payment would be based on a rate of 10% (the final 1% reduction in the 3-2-1 buydown). In years 4 through 30, the payment would be based on an interest rate of 11%.

I'm sure that this scenario sounds a lot better than paying 13% interest for all 30 years of your loan. However, what the homebuyers did not know is that these builders were paying a fortune for this "special financing" – and building these insane costs into the price of their homes.

I worked for a large, national builder and saw their "spec sheet". This was a detailed list of homes that had already been completed or were currently under construction. The builder was paying 25-28% in points to buy down the interest rate. This means that for a $200,000 home, the value of the home itself was around $150,000 – the other $50,000 was the cost of buying down the interest rate!

What do you think happened when interest rates naturally fell down to around 8%? The "value" of that special financing evaporated and the homeowner was left owing close to $200,000 on a house worth $150,000. What do you think comes next? Correct – a rush of people walking away from their homes and their mortgage payments.

Interestingly, the homebuyer had the option to take the cost of buying down the interest rate as a discount off the price of the home and accept the market interest rate at the time. But who did that? No one that I can think of.

An associate and I ran some calculations at that time and we concluded that a homebuyer would be dollars ahead if they were to take the discount and get a negative amortization loan. Payments would have been lower and the addition to principal would still have been less than that extreme overpayment for the home in the first place.

That would only have been a temporary solution, of course, and this example was really just to illustrate how bad it was to increase the price of the homes by that much, just to offer a financing package that would soon become worthless anyway.

It actually would have made more sense for a homebuyer to take the discount and either accept an adjustable rate mortgage, which would have drifted downward with prevailing rates, or even just refinance their fixed rate later – maybe even more than once – as rates declined. I think a lot of people learned an expensive lesson during that time.

Regulations now prevent something like this from happening again, as regulators have now imposed a limit on how many points can be spent on financing without being backed out of the value during the appraisal process. They have also cracked down on manipulated appraisals – that's a different story that I will not take the time to go into here.

Example #2. Much more recently, I had a financially savvy homebuyer who wanted to refinance his mortgage to a Jumbo 7/1 ARM, which was not a bad idea in his case. He was enamored with the idea of an interest rate below 3%. I gave him my honest opinion that it would not be the best idea to pay a bunch of points to buy down the rate, as this was simply pre-paying interest – and if he happened to sell the house before a rather long break-even period, he would lose money by doing this.

He insisted that he was going to stay in the house and keep this mortgage for years so that it would pay off in the end. A few months later, he called me and said "guess what?" They had decided to sell the house and buy another home – which, again, was not a bad idea in his case. The only unfortunate thing was that almost all of the money he spent to buy down that interest rate was now wasted. The loan was paid off only a few months after closing. He would have been better off with the higher rate and lower costs.

Again, there may very well be a good reason to prepay interest by buying down your interest rate. But, at least make sure that you have looked at the break-even period and still think it makes sense to do so. Here's how to do that:

1. Find out how much it will cost to buy down the rate.

2. Find out how much you will save in your monthly payment if you buy down the rate.

3. Divide the upfront cost in #1 by the monthly savings in #2. That will give you the number of months it will take to recoup your "investment" in buying down that rate.

4. Note that this does not take into consideration the ***time value of money***. Because of inflation, each dollar that you pay right now to buy down

the interest rate is worth more than each dollar that you will save in the future due to the lower rate.

So, in "real" dollars, it will take a little longer than your computed break-even period to recoup your investment. If there's any significant chance that you will sell or refinance before that break-even date arrives, you might want to think twice about buying down the rate.

5. This break-even period calculation also does not take into consideration the *opportunity cost* of tying up your cash in buying down the interest rate.

    What else could you do with that money? Is there an investment that you could make that would offer a reasonable to good return? You will lose that return if your money is not available to put into that other opportunity because you spent it buying down your interest rate. Just something to consider.

Okay, that's my two cents' worth on buying down the interest rate. Not always a bad idea, but you should at least think it through first.

15

ESCROWING FOR TAXES & INSURANCE

When you buy a home, you are responsible for paying property taxes and homeowner's insurance. These are usually paid once per year. Property tax is paid around the end of each year and is paid in arrears. When the year is at its end, you pay the tax due for that year.

Homeowner's insurance is paid in advance, usually each year but sometimes every six months. Plan on paying for your first year of homeowner's insurance, in advance, as part of your cash-to-close.

This cost is usually included in what is generally referred to as "closing costs", but you can pay for this directly if you prefer, as long as it is done before you close on your home purchase. After you have owned your home for one year, you will need to pay the second year's policy premium, also in advance.

An *escrow account* helps to even out these expenses by allowing (and requiring) you to pay 1/12 of your annual property tax and homeowner's insurance bill every month, so that after making payments for a full year, there is sufficient money in your escrow account to pay for these annual expenses. This is basically a forced savings account to make sure you have the money when those bills are due.

When you open an escrow account, usually at the same time you are closing on the purchase of your home, you need to put a couple of months' worth of payments in there so that there is a small cushion. There are a few reasons why this is a good idea.

For example, the bank or mortgage company that administers your escrow account while servicing your mortgage may make their annual property tax payments before you make your last payment for the year. There needs to be enough money in the account to allow for that.

Also, taxes and insurance rates seem to go up more often than they go down. It's always a good idea to have a little bit of a buffer in there to reduce the probability and/or pain of an *escrow shortage*.

If your tax or insurance rates go up and you continue to pay the old amount, you could wind up with a shortage of funds in your escrow account, and that will have to be remedied. It may not be any fun for you to find out that your payments have gone way up until you catch up on your escrow shortfall.

Here's another reason why you need to put some money in your escrow account to get things started. When you rent a home, your monthly rental payments are generally paid in advance. Mortgage loan payments are made in arrears. That means that when you move out of a rental and into a home that you have purchased, you will naturally get to skip your housing payment for one month.

For example, if you move out of your apartment and into your new home on January 31st, there is no February housing payment. This is because you paid your January rent on or around January 1st but your February housing expense payment isn't due until March 1st. When the month is over, you pay for that month. This is because interest is paid every month as it accrues – interest has accrued after that month has gone by, not before that month has started.

So, in addition to the 2 months' taxes and insurance payments that need to be initially placed into your escrow account, there is another month that goes by where your taxes and insurance need to be covered. That means you should probably be prepared to put around 3 months' worth of taxes and insurance into your new escrow account.

In practice, they may only collect for 2 months – or maybe 3 months' taxes and 2 months' insurance – to start your escrow account, but it is not a bad idea to be prepared for a little more, just in case that is necessary.

Remember that this is in addition to the first year of insurance that you have to pay for upfront. When you pay for your first year of homeowner's insurance, that covers you for one year. When you put 2-3 months' insurance premiums into your escrow account, all that money does is sit in your escrow account, waiting for more money to arrive every month so that when your first year is up, there is enough money in that account to pay for your second year's premium.

So, you probably ought to be prepared to pay for about 15 months' worth of homeowner's insurance upfront. 12 months will be paid to the insurance company at closing to cover your first year and the rest will be placed in your escrow account to start saving for your second year's advance payment.

Fortunately, property taxes don't work that way because they are paid in arrears. You still need to put some money into your escrow account to start with, so that there is enough in there when your end-of-year tax payment is made, but at least you don't have to pay for a full year upfront, in addition to the amount deposited into your escrow account.

Since property taxes are due after the year has gone by, what happens if you close on your home purchase at some point during the year other than on January 1st? That means you did not own the home for the entire year. Do you have to pay for the entire year's taxes?

No. The seller of the home will have to put up the pro-rated tax amount into your escrow account, covering the time that the seller owned the home. If you close on your home on July 1st, for example, the seller will have to provide ½ of that year's property tax amount so that when taxes are due at the end of the year, you will have the money to pay for the entire year – but *you* only had to pay for your fair share.

There are a couple more things I need to explain in this section. While we're talking about loading your escrow account with money to prime the pump, so to speak, there are limits. An escrow account is only allowed to keep a certain amount of extra funds at any given time. (We'll let the computers calculate that amount using formulas that only they seem to know.) If there is too much money in there, they will have to send you an ***escrow refund***.

To make sure they don't go over the limit initially, there is very often an ***aggregate adjustment*** that is credited toward your cash-to-close amount before closing. This is because the estimate of how much money you need to load into your escrow account initially often exceeds that limit and the excess must be refunded to you.

Here's another thing you should know. An escrow account is generally optional if you are putting at least 20% down. If you are using a conventional loan and you are putting 20% down or more, you can choose to waive the escrow account.

The lender may punish you a little bit for waiving escrows, by increasing your pricing just slightly – usually only about 12 ½ bps. The reason for this is that there is always a small risk that, at the end of the year, you won't have the money to pay those taxes. And if you don't pay them, the lender has the privilege of doing so.

Your lender does not want to lose their investment by allowing the local taxing authority to foreclose on your home. If the lender has to foreclose, they will foreclose – but in the meantime, those property taxes are going to get paid. And yes, they will be coming after you to recover those taxes – and if you don't reimburse them, you'll be out looking for a rental again. "No pay, no stay."

A FHA loan requires an escrow account no matter what, so you don't need to worry about whether or not you should waive escrows. As for VA loans, the Department of Veterans Affairs does not require an escrow account on VA loans – but your lender might.

If you have an FHA loan or put less than 20% down on a conventional loan, you are probably paying a monthly mortgage insurance (MI) premium. This monthly amount will also be part of your escrow account, though you won't have to pay 2 or 3 months' worth of the premiums upfront. It's just good to know where that money is going and what your escrow balance consists of when you see the statement.

For most people, an escrow account is probably a good idea – it will help to make sure that your property taxes and homeowner's insurance are budgeted for and paid on time. If you are highly financially disciplined *and* have ways of earning money on the funds that would otherwise be sitting in your escrow account earning nothing all year, you may choose to waive the escrow account. Otherwise, I would suggest avoiding the year-end stress by using an escrow account.

16

PRO-RATED INTEREST

Mortgage payments are always due on the first of the month (although you will generally have a 15-day grace period before a late penalty is assessed). So, if you close on your loan at some time other than the first day of the month, there will be pro-rated interest until the end of that month. This pro-rated interest will be included in what is generally referred to as "closing costs", along with your escrow deposits and other costs. Here's how the timing works.

Let's say that you are closing on your new home on January 20th. Your pro-rated interest will cover the 12 days from January 20th through January 31st. (For those of you who are curious, this will be 1/12 of your annual interest rate multiplied by your initial loan amount, divided by the number of days in that month, then multiplied by the number of days starting with your closing date and ending with the last day in that calendar month.)

So if you close in the middle of the month, your pro-rated interest is your mortgage payment for that partial month. Then the next month – your first full calendar month – there is no payment because mortgage payments are made in arrears. So, in this example, pro-rated interest covered January, there's no payment in February, and your regular monthly mortgage payments start on March 1st.

If you close within the first few days (usually 5) of the month, you may elect to skip the pro-rated interest for that month and start on your regular monthly payments at the first of the upcoming month. That means that the month in which you close is the month that you do not have a mortgage payment, as you will be making a payment at the beginning of the following month.

For example, if you close on January 3rd, and do not want to pay pro-rated interest between January 3rd and January 31st, instead of your first payment being due on March 1st, your first payment would be due on February 1st. This option is called a ***short pay***.

17

LOAN-TO-VALUE, HOUSING RATIO, DEBT RATIO

There are a few ratios that are very useful to be familiar with when you are buying (or refinancing) a home. The first one is the ***Loan-To-Value***, or ***LTV***.

The LTV (loan-to-value) is the percentage (often shown as a decimal) of the value or purchase price of a property that is being financed, or that is presently owed on the property. (When you are purchasing the home, if the purchase price and appraised value are not equal, they generally use the lower of the two.)

For example, if you are buying a $200,000 home and putting $40,000 down, your LTV is 80% or 0.80. If you put 20% down on a home in the past but have made payments for a few years, your initial LTV was 80% but it has probably come down to 60% or 70% or something like that.

Two things will affect this change in your LTV:

1. You have been paying toward your principal balance with your monthly payments;
2. The value of your home has most likely gone up during time that you have owned it.

Here's how the numbers work:

Mortgage Balance ÷ Value of Home = LTV

100% (Value of Home) − LTV % = Equity %

Example: If your home is worth $200,000 right now, and your mortgage balance is $150,000:

$150,000 ÷ $200,000 = 75% LTV

100% (Value) − 75% (LTV) = 25% (Equity)

In dollars, that means…

$200,000 (Value) − $150,000 (Mortgage Balance) = $50,000 (Equity)

When you are trying to get a mortgage, the loan-to-value ratio is important because this number affects your interest rate, is part of loan program parameters, and will probably determine whether or not mortgage insurance is required.

The next two ratios are related to each other and most often considered together in determining whether you will qualify for a certain loan amount under a specific loan program. These two ratios are the Housing Ratio and the Debt Ratio.

The **Housing Ratio**, also known as the *front ratio* or *top ratio*, expresses as a percentage (or decimal) how much of your gross monthly income is being used to cover your "housing expense" in a given scenario. Your housing expense will include:

- Principal and Interest payment
- Property Tax – monthly amount, whether escrowed or not
- Homeowner's Insurance – monthly amount, whether escrowed or not
- Mortgage Insurance – monthly amount, if applicable
- HOA/Condo Fees – monthly amount, if applicable, even though not part of your mortgage payment

For example, let's say that your "useable" gross monthly income (as determined by underwriting process) is $8,000. And your total mortgage payment (including PITI+MI) is $1,900. In addition, you pay $300/quarter in HOA dues. (That's $100/mo.) So, your total housing expense is $2,000/mo.

Housing Expense ÷ Gross Income = Housing Ratio

$2,000 ÷ $8,000 = 25%

Housing Ratio = 25%

That is a reasonable housing ratio. Acceptable qualifying ratios are generally considered to be 28/36, meaning that your housing ratio should not exceed 28% of your gross monthly income and your debt ratio should not exceed 36% of your gross monthly income.

Though these are the standard numbers, this varies widely and many programs right now are much more lenient than this. The debt ratio seems to be the number they are stricter on most of the time, though the housing ratio definitely has its limits.

The **Debt Ratio** is also known as the *back ratio* or *bottom ratio*, but seems to be most often referred to as the **debt-to-income ratio** or **DTI**. This ratio includes the housing ratio plus other monthly debt service.

What this means is that if you have borrowed money and are making monthly payments to repay this debt, the amount of these monthly payments is included in this DTI ratio.

Sometimes, an amount will be included even if you are not making payments, such as student loan payments that may be presently deferred. In addition, automobile lease payments will be treated as if this were repayment of a debt. A monthly child support or spousal support obligation is also included in this ratio.

Not included in the DTI (debt ratio) are expenses such as utility bills, auto insurance premiums, cable, cell phone, grocery expenses, etc., as these expenses are (usually) not repayment of money that has been borrowed and must be repaid.

Of course, if you put these expenses on your credit card and you carry a balance on that card, the minimum payment will be included in your DTI.

Some **installment** loan debt (*"closed-end"* loans that do not include the option to run the balance back up during the repayment period, unlike *"open-end"* or **revolving** accounts such as credit cards) may be removed from your DTI if there are 10 or fewer payments remaining. Check with your loan officer regarding these types of details.

Returning to the example above, let's say that your gross income is $8,000/month and your housing expense (total mortgage payment + HOA dues) is $2,000. In addition, you have the following monthly debt payments:

- $500 car payment
- $300 installment loan payment
- $100 Nordstrom minimum payment
- $50 Visa minimum payment
- $50 MasterCard minimum payment

So, your total monthly non-housing debt service is $1,000. That means that your housing ratio will be $2,000 / $8,000 and your DTI will be $3,000 / $8,000. Therefore, your ratios will look like this:

25.0% / 37.5%

This means that your housing ratio is 25% of your gross monthly income and your debt ratio (DTI) is 37.5% of your gross monthly income. These are good ratios. Even conventional loans will approve higher ratios than this right now.

Even though the traditional standard ratios are 28/36, debt ratios of 39%, 45%, and even 55% are now acceptable, depending on the type of loan. With the expansion of qualifying ratios, a borrower's debt ratio seem to be a more important consideration than the housing ratio, though the housing ratio is definitely considered. I have done FHA loans with debt ratios well into the 50's, though they will still limit the housing ratio somewhere in the 40's.

I should emphasize here that I am not trying to train you to be your own loan officer. This book will not go anywhere near that level of detail, and will not even approach certain subjects that would probably not be useful to you as a mortgage borrower.

I am simply trying to help those of you who would like to know more about the mortgage process to be better-educated borrowers, so that you can understand what is happening and make the best decisions possible throughout the process.

If you find any part of this book to be boring or confusing, just put it down and call a good loan officer for assistance. Please don't feel like you have to learn all of this information before you should consider buying a home – that is definitely not the case.

18

CLOSING COSTS

This is an area of confusion for a few reasons. First of all, what is really considered to be a closing cost? In the past, I have noticed certain loan officers quote closing costs that appear to be quite low – suspiciously low, in fact. Usually, there are two possible reasons for this.

First, maybe the term "closing costs" was not used in a very all-inclusive manner. Perhaps pre-paid property taxes, homeowner's insurance and pro-rated interest were not included in that total. Maybe, in an informal phone call, only the lender fees were mentioned.

Closing Costs might be defined in a variety of ways but, in my observation, borrowers aren't nearly as concerned with how the costs are classified, or the actual break down of the total amount, as they are with how much money they are going to have to come up with, in addition to their down payment.

So, let's go through what you, the borrower, will most likely want included in a total amount when you ask a loan officer how much your closing costs will be. I like to separate these costs into three categories, and you will probably want all three to be included in your total:

(1) ***Lender Fees***. This will include charges for underwriting and processing. There may be other things as well, but what you really want to know is how much the lender is charging you to do your loan. If you are paying points to buy down the rate, that would also be included here, but this would generally be your choice.

(2) ***Non-Lender Fees***. This will include things like the appraisal, title insurance, recording fees, property survey (if required), attorney fees, settlement fees, title endorsements, etc. Some of these are often referred to as "junk fees", but since they are necessary, I prefer to think of them as "necessary evils".

(3) ***Pre-Paids & Impounds***. *Property taxes* and *homeowner's insurance* need to be paid whether you get a mortgage or not. *Pro-rated interest* simply takes the place of an initial, pro-rated mortgage payment so that all mortgages can be due at the first of the month.

These expenses can easily be left out of someone's definition of closing costs. But, they still have to be paid when you close on your home, so I'm guessing that you want to know how much this will all add up to.

When you get a written estimate of these fees, it should be all-inclusive and fairly accurate. When you get a formal document called a **_Loan Estimate_**, or **_LE_**, it will show a breakdown and total. There are restrictions on how much these fees may increase once they are disclosed, so the LE should be pretty close to your final number.

When you ask a loan officer how much your closing costs will be, make sure they are including non-lender fees and all your taxes, insurance, etc. – even the first year's insurance that is generally paid at closing. No, the lender is not getting that money, but you still want to know how much you will need in order to close on your home.

If you want to compare lender fees, then you can ask about lender fees, specifically. If you ask the lender how much your closing costs will be and he/she says something like "$1,250", that is most likely the lender fee only – the title insurance alone is probably more than that (though that is often paid by the seller).

The second reason why your closing costs might seem lower than normal is that they might have premium-priced your loan. We covered this in the section on how pricing works. If you are more sensitive to closing costs than you are to interest rates, a loan officer may be quoting you an interest rate that is above par, so that accepting that interest rate entitles you to receive a credit toward your closing costs.

This is not necessarily a bad thing. However, if you are the type of consumer that wants to be educated on the mortgage process badly enough that you are still reading this book, you may want to know your options and make that decision for yourself.

The fact is, closing costs really should not vary that much between lenders. All these costs need to be covered, and they generally cost about the same amount wherever you go.

If I quote you $7,000 and someone else quotes you $1,500, I can promise you that they are either leaving something out that I have included, or they are premium-pricing your loan. I'm not saying they are bad, I'm only suggesting that if you are reading this book, you will probably want to know what's going on with your closing costs.

19

HOW TO CHOOSE A LENDER

This is a sensitive issue and I'm sure to offend somebody in this section. Apologies in advance – I do not mean anything personal against any specific person, their company, or their situation. That said, I'd rather be honest and help you, than be overly nice and not help you.

In any profession, some practitioners are better than others. The mortgage business is much more complicated than it seems like it should be. Many new people are not trained adequately and have to learn by making mistakes. But, when mistakes are made on *you*, you may not be happy.

I have seen the domino effect happen, where at the last minute the underwriter decides she can't close on your loan. Your loan was supposed to close tomorrow. Now, you have one day to go out and find a rental for your family because you are already obligated to leave your present home.

In addition, the seller of the home you were trying to buy can no longer close on the home that they were trying to buy – which causes that family a multitude of problems. And the seller of your seller's prospective home is also faced with a set of problems they did not anticipate.

Yes, I am thinking of a real situation that actually happened in the past. It was like a train wreck – from a nightmare – with zombies – and giant spiders – and ugly people. I hope I never witness anything like that ever again.

I will fill you in on my experience, and you can do with it whatever you like. I hope that the problems I talk about here have already been corrected so that these things are no longer a valid concern – but I do not believe that to be the case as of yet, at least not substantially.

I worked for the big banks for a number of years. Yes, those big banks – with mortgage companies. I always wondered why Realtors, in general, were so vehemently opposed to their clients trying to get a mortgage through one of those big banks. I thought it was an unfair judgment based on a few, isolated instances.

Well, after working for several of those big banks for long enough to identify a pattern of neglect and abuse, I hereby apologize to all of you Realtors out there – I am sorry to have to admit that you were right all along.

The horror stories I could tell you would make your hair stand up and frizz out (and melt your face off, while I'm on a roll of exaggerated visuals). I believe that the big banks probably don't really want to be in the mortgage business – one of their CEO's even said publicly that he wished he could get out of the mortgage business. And if they can't figure out how to do it well, I think they should get out. So, why are they still in the mortgage business?

One of the big banks that I worked for did a study and they determined that, if they could get a customer to have two key bank products, that – on average – that customer would wind up with more than eight bank products from their bank, thereby successfully "owning" that customer and preventing competing banks from getting that customer's business. What were those two products? A checking account and a mortgage.

Banks want assets. They want all your money, all the time. And I don't hate banks, by the way. I have worked for three of the "big four" and I still have some type of account(s) with each of them. Interestingly, when the fourth one called me to offer me a position, I politely declined and explained that I had decided I no longer wanted to work for a big bank – and the manager I was speaking with "completely understood". Yeah... they know...

Anyway, banks want assets. And they use the mortgage account to get assets. It's like this. Let's say that you presently bank with Bank #1. Now, you're looking for a mortgage. Bank #2 offers you a discount on your closing costs or rate/pricing if you will move $100,000 or $250,000 from Bank #1 over to Bank #2. (Yeah, they're not too interested in your $20, they want big accounts.)

If they can get you to move a big account from your bank to their bank, it's worth offering you an incentive to do so – because now, they own your business. You start moving away from Bank #1, because you have a big account – and your mortgage – at Bank #2. Now, when you need a bank for some reason, which bank are you most likely to think of?

Big banks know that if they let a competing bank get your mortgage, they are likely to lose the rest of your business as well. So, if a big bank stopped doing mortgages, they would surely lose business to some other big bank that is still doing mortgages. And that is why they want to do your mortgage.

A well-known, rapidly growing, newer bank decided that they should also be in the mortgage business a relatively short time ago. Now, just recently, I heard the announcement that this bank has decided to exit the mortgage business. I applaud this decision. If you can't do it right, please don't torture the customers any longer. But I have to wonder how this will affect their growth.

This commentary is my opinion, by the way, based on my personal experience. However, the fact that they really, really want big accounts is also evidenced by their interest rates and incentives.

Jumbo loans generally have higher interest rates than conforming loans do. But big banks, at least at certain times, offer jumbo loans with lower rates than their smaller, conforming loans offer. And they offer incentives – tied to a new mortgage – for large account holders to move their assets over to that bank. This is one way that they can attract those higher net worth customers.

A customer purchasing a $950,000 home using a jumbo loan (which generally requires a large down payment) is likely to have a larger savings account than a first-time homebuyer putting the minimum down on a $150,000 home purchase, using a FHA loan. So, if their objective is to get to those big accounts, which mortgage customer will they go after more aggressively?

Again, I'm not saying that this is bad – it's probably a

smart idea. The problem is that, in my observation, compared to a "legitimate" mortgage company (that just does mortgages), there is a much higher risk that your loan won't close once it gets to your closing date – and that you will have been subjected to a variety of inhumane torture techniques during the process of getting to that point, so that it will be particularly painful when your loan does not close.

I have seen this repeatedly and consistently over my years working for the big banks, which is why I had to change teams, so to speak. I'll spare you more specifics so that we can move on. My point is that it actually does matter which type of organization you are getting your mortgage from.

Like I said before, the mortgage business is much more complex than it seems like it should be. There are many moving parts, and one little change can cause a domino effect that you may not enjoy. Some types of companies are better set up to offer the kind of quality service that you expect than others are.

My preference, for the best possible customer experience, is a non-bank mortgage company that is not a national call center. I work for such a company now, and I am familiar with other, similar companies which also strive to offer competitive prices and a much better customer experience than do alternatives of lesser quality. The type of company you get your mortgage from matters.

The individual loan officer and his/her support team also matter. Many times, a new loan officer is welcomed aboard, given an office or cubicle, and wished good luck. Support may be available, but supervision weak. This new L.O. may have great potential, but is doomed to learn the business from his/her mistakes.

You do not want to be one of those mistakes. So, and I say this hesitantly, you may be best off working with a L.O. that has at least several years' experience. Or, if you're working with a newer L.O., at least make sure that there is great managerial and processing support so that preventable mistakes are not made on your file. No offense to newer mortgage professionals, but there is a learning curve and I've seen a lot of mistakes.

If you are working with an experienced, successful Realtor, and this Realtor has a long-standing relationship with a particular loan officer, there is probably a reason for that. You may want to listen to what your Realtor suggests.

Your Realtor wants your transaction to close, perhaps almost as badly as you do. She is going to recommend a loan officer that she has reason to believe will help to make this happen – and with the least drama possible.

If your Realtor says to stay away from a particular

bank, or big banks in general, or if (s)he suggests that you ignore those teaser rates you see advertised online from the call-center mortgage companies, I would suggest heeding that advice.

20

GET YOUR DOCUMENTS READY

It's always good to know how to be prepared for whatever you are trying to accomplish. When you decide that it is time to think seriously about investing in your own home, the first thing to do is not to call a Realtor and go look at homes. Most Realtors do not want to waste your time or theirs by looking at homes when they have no idea what price range you should be looking at – or if you can even qualify for a mortgage at all.

In addition, if you did manage to find a home and make a written offer, the seller will probably not consider that offer if it is not accompanied by a ***Pre-Approval Letter*** from a lender (unless it is a cash offer that is not subject to loan approval).

In addition, when there are multiple offers on the same property, as is the current situation in my location, which lender has issued your pre-approval letter is also a factor in which offer will be accepted. The seller's Realtor has a pretty good idea of which companies issue pre-approval letters that are likely to not be worth the paper they are printed on.

So, the first thing you want to do is to apply for a mortgage somewhere. If you know or are in contact with a good Realtor already, you may ask your Realtor for a good lender referral. If not, you can call a few successful Realtors in your area and ask who they recommend. If you happen to be purchasing a home in the great State of Texas, please feel free to contact me personally.

Once you have found a lender that you are interested in working with, you might start with an online application, or do one over the phone or in person with that loan officer – however you are comfortable.

While that L.O. (loan officer) is working up some numbers and a pre-approval for you, you will want to get some documents together. These documents are not going to be the only things that you are asked to provide during the loan process, but they are a good start.

The list below applies to all borrowers who will be on the mortgage application:

1. Last 30 days pay stubs (if W2 employee)

2. Last 2 years W2s (if W2 employee)

3. Last 2 years 1099s (if you have Schedule C income)

4. Last 2 years personal tax returns (and business entity tax returns, if applicable) including all schedules (if you have self-employment or 1099 income, own investment real estate, or if at least 25% of your W2 income comes from commissions.)

    - (Note that if you own at least 25% of your company, you will be considered to be self-employed, even if you get a W2.)

5. Year-to-Date Profit & Loss Statement (Income Statement) and Balance Sheet (if self-employed)

6. Last 2 months bank/asset account statements for all accounts being considered as part of the qualifying process

7. Property tax and property insurance statements/information for any real estate that you own and will continue to own after closing on your home purchase.

Your loan officer will give you a list of the documents needed in your particular case, but it would be a good idea to get started putting together the items listed above as a starting point.

Also note that the initial list of required documents that you are given in order to start the mortgage process will probably not be the end of it. As the process moves forward, the lender will determine what other items they may also need before they can close on your loan.

Please do not be frustrated if the lender asks you for more documentation during the loan process – this is normal (within reason) and should be expected as part of the process of getting your loan closed.

It is also useful to know that not all buyers have to be on the mortgage. For example, let's say that one spouse has all or most of the income, and also has a better credit score than the other spouse. This couple can purchase the home jointly, so that both spouses are on the title and have legal ownership of the home, with only the more qualified spouse applying for the mortgage. That is perfectly fine and happens all the time.

Just remember that if you want your income to be considered for qualifying purposes, your credit score will also be considered. And lenders use the lowest ***mid-score*** (whichever of the three scores falls in the middle) of all applicants as the official credit score for qualifying purposes.

It is also important to know that if you are applying for a FHA loan and you are the only spouse on the loan, only your income will be considered – but any debts that are in your spouse's name will also be considered in your debt-to-income ratio.

There are also some strict guidelines regarding student loan payments, even if those payments are presently deferred. Make sure to go over these details with your loan officer if you think they might apply to your situation.

21

THE LOAN ESTIMATE (LE) AND CLOSING DISCLOSURE (CD)

Recent changes in the way the mortgage process is regulated have resulted in a couple of new documents that you will see on your way to closing on your new home. These documents attempt to make clearer information that was previously included on separate documents that have now been discontinued.

You may be familiar with the previous documents, the Good Faith Estimate (GFE) and the Truth-in-Lending Disclosure (TIL). These are important documents about the costs involved in obtaining mortgage financing.

Under the new regulations referred to as ***TRID***, these two documents are combined into one document called the ***Loan Estimate (LE)***. Lenders are required to send this LE to you within 3 business days of receiving a certain set of details from you which legally constitute a *mortgage application*.

TRID stands for the ***TILA-RESPA Integrated Disclosure rule***. (TILA = Truth in Lending Act; RESPA = Real Estate Settlement Procedures Act, in case anyone cares.)

You might also be familiar with two other documents known as the Final Truth-in-Lending Statement (Final TIL) and the HUD-1 Settlement Statement. These were the final documents issued at closing time, which explain all the final costs, APR, etc. Under TRID, these two documents have also been combined into one new final document known as the ***Closing Disclosure (CD)***.

This is a very simplified explanation of TRID, the LE and the CD. There are many more details that you probably have no interest in learning about, but it is a good idea to know what the LE and the CD are when it comes time to deal with those documents.

We will not go into the specific line items included in these documents here. I would encourage you to go over these things with your loan officer, if you want to have a good understanding of the specific items included in these two important documents.

22

DOWN PAYMENT ASSISTANCE PROGRAMS (DPA)

What happens if you believe that you are ready to own a home but you have not saved an adequate amount of money to cover your down payment and closing costs? There are **DPA (*down payment assistance*)** programs that may be able to help.

There are many different programs that apply to many different geographical areas and these programs can change fairly frequently. I will not attempt to address specific programs here, but I will give you a basic idea of how they might work. If you want more specific information, you should find a loan officer who works with DPA programs.

One type of DPA program would work like this. An organization raises money through the sale of a bond issue (debt) in order to assist prospective homebuyers with their down payments. In other words, the organization borrows money and issues IOUs (bonds) as evidence of their obligation to repay this debt with interest. The money raised is then gifted to qualifying homebuyers.

Because this debt has to be repaid by the organization, they have to have some source of revenue. If you are the recipient of one of these down payment gifts, your interest rate will probably be significantly higher than the market rate. This means that over time you will, in effect, be repaying that initial assistance by making a higher monthly payment.

In addition, there is usually a fee imposed upon homebuyers who receive this down payment gift. Between the interest rate markup and the fees, the organization has the funds to repay the debt and retire the bonds.

These types of programs may currently be under attack, to some extent, because it could be argued that, in actuality, the homebuyer is borrowing the down payment and paying it back monthly through the higher payment associated with this "premium-priced" loan.

My opinion is this: if you can come up with the down payment on your own (or through a family gift), that would be preferable. But if you cannot do this, or cannot do it quickly enough, this program might be very good for you. Just make sure that you are not getting into something you cannot afford.

If you have no discretionary income right now, so that you cannot save for your down payment, you need to think twice about taking on homeownership and all of the related expenses involved. It may be that some adjustments in your personal finances should be considered first. Just make sure that you are not setting yourself up for a future foreclosure.

Another type of DPA program offers more competitive interest rates, and the down payment assistance actually comes in the form of a small loan that is secured by the property, but in a junior position to your mortgage. Your regular mortgage would be a 1st mortgage and the DPA loan would be a 2nd mortgage.

You may never have to repay this loan, and you will probably not have any monthly payments or interest charges. You will need to be familiar with the details of this program before you participate, so that there are no surprises later. This type of DPA program may also be a good choice for you as the interest rate may be more reasonable.

There are also other types of programs that could help, from local down payment grants sponsored by your city, to a program that converts some of your tax-deductible interest to an actual tax credit, potentially saving you some money and reducing your monthly payment for qualifying purposes.

There are qualifications for these programs. The required credit score will probably exceed the FHA minimum score. You will have to earn enough money to qualify for the loan – but you cannot exceed a predetermined maximum for your program, family size and area (for many programs).

You might even have to be a "first-time homebuyer", which is defined as someone who has not owned a home in the past three years. Check with a good loan officer for options and specifics.

Another option to consider would be a ***USDA*** loan. This type of loan is sponsored by the ***United States Department of Agriculture*** and requires that you purchase a home located in a designated rural area. You may also hear this referred to as a ***Rural Development Loan (RD Loan)***.

There are qualifying requirements to be aware of, such as a higher minimum credit score than with a FHA loan. But, if you qualify, you can finance 100% of the value/price of the home. There is an upfront funding fee and a small monthly MI (mortgage insurance) payment required on these loans, but this will probably be quite a bit less expensive than the upfront plus monthly MI required on a FHA loan.

23

SHOULD YOU REFINANCE?

Maybe. That depends on whether the refinance will save you more than it costs you – or, if there are other reasons that make the expense worthwhile. There are actually a number of reasons to refinance and, even if it costs you money, your reason may justify the expense.

If there is no compelling reason that you need to refinance, and you are simply thinking that it might save you money to do so, make sure you compare the cost versus the benefit. Here's a rather obvious example:

You have been in your home for 5-7 years and the initial fixed interest rate period of your 5/1 or 7/1 ARM is coming to an end. When you bought your home, you were sure that you were not going to stay very long, so you got an adjustable rate mortgage for the lower initial period interest rate.

But, things have changed since then and you now intend to own the home long-term. An ARM is no longer attractive to you as a long-term option, interest rates are low, and you can premium-price a refinance at an attractive rate with almost no closing costs. Easy decision.

Next example, you now have a 30-year fixed mortgage and have been paying on it for about 10 years. You think you'll be there for another 10-15 at least and interest rates are just a little bit lower than they were when you got your mortgage. You are not sure whether the monthly savings will justify the expense. Let's say that you would save $69 per month and the cost would be $5,000 if you get another 30 year fixed loan.

Things to consider:

- Your break-even time would be:

    $5,000 ÷ $69 = 72$ months, or 6 years.

- Is it worth putting up $5,000 right now if you won't even get your full investment back until 6 years has gone by? And the dollars you do get back are gradually decreasing in value over that time? Maybe, if you are going to be in the house for a lot longer than that and you don't really have anything better to do with the money, so that you are not concerned with the opportunity cost. But is there a better option to look at?

- You have to remember that with the above scenario you are extending your mortgage payoff out another 10 years, and overall, this is likely to more than outweigh the benefits of the monthly savings. I would hesitate to do this without some other compelling reason.

- Here's an idea: Can you afford to make a higher monthly payment than you have been paying for the past 10 years? After all, your income has gone up, some expenses have gone away, you're more comfortable now – maybe so.

  o What would happen if you considered refinancing with a 20-year loan instead of a 30-year loan? First, you would not be extending your mortgage payoff another 10 years past your currently scheduled payoff time.

  o Second, your interest rate would probably be a little lower than the 30-year loan you're looking at, so that could increase the benefit for refinancing. You can ask your loan officer to calculate how much interest you will save by doing the refinance.

  o Better yet, can you afford the higher payment associated with refinancing to a 15-year fixed loan? There is a much better interest rate break when you go to a 15-year loan. So, the payments will be higher, but you'll save a lot more interest in the long run.

o Don't forget that your current loan probably allows for pre-payment without a penalty. That means that you could simulate switching to a 15-year fixed loan simply by calculating how much your monthly payment will need to be in order to have your loan paid off in 15 years.

Then compare that scenario with having the lower rate of actually refinancing the loan to that 15-year fixed mortgage. Is it worth the cost of refinancing? Maybe – you have to run the numbers to find out. I would ask your loan officer for help with this.

- A loan officer has to be able to justify doing a refinance. There must be a "benefit to the borrower". That means that unless there is some other reason why you need to refinance, we have to be able to show that the numbers are in your favor – that for the length of time you anticipate staying in the house, the refinance will save you money.

If you really need a lower monthly payment, we can refinance to a longer term – because that solves a problem. If you just want to save interest overall, we can reduce your interest rate and your term – even when that results in a higher monthly payment. You just need to be comfortable with the new payment.

- There is no way to address here every possible scenario that might cause you to think about a refinance, so I'm not even going to try. I just hope that I've given you a few things to think about, and that you will work with a competent and honest loan officer when you are considering a refinance for any reason.

24

WHAT IS AN AMORTIZATION SCHEDULE?

An *amortization schedule* shows you the breakdown of each payment you make on your mortgage – how much goes to principal, how much to interest, and how much you still owe on the mortgage after each payment is made. Here is an example of an amortization schedule for a $200,000 loan amount at 4.5% interest fixed for 30 years:

Payment Date	Payment	Principal	Interest	Balance
Mar 2018	$1,013.37	$263.37	$750.00	$199,736.63
Apr 2018	$1,013.37	$264.36	$749.01	$199,472.27
May 2018	$1,013.37	$265.35	$748.02	$199,206.92
Jun 2018	$1,013.37	$266.34	$747.03	$198,940.58

Payment Date	Payment	Principal	Interest	Balance
Jul 2018	$1,013.37	$267.34	$746.03	$198,673.23
Aug 2018	$1,013.37	$268.35	$745.02	$198,404.89
Sep 2018	$1,013.37	$269.35	$744.02	$198,135.54
Oct 2018	$1,013.37	$270.36	$743.01	$197,865.17
Nov 2018	$1,013.37	$271.38	$741.99	$197,593.80
Dec 2018	$1,013.37	$272.39	$740.98	$197,321.40
Jan 2019	$1,013.37	$273.42	$739.96	$197,047.99
Feb 2019	$1,013.37	$274.44	$738.93	$196,773.55
Mar 2019	$1,013.37	$275.47	$737.90	$196,498.08
Apr 2019	$1,013.37	$276.50	$736.87	$196,221.57
May 2019	$1,013.37	$277.54	$735.83	$195,944.03
Jun 2019	$1,013.37	$278.58	$734.79	$195,665.45
Jul 2019	$1,013.37	$279.63	$733.75	$195,385.83
Aug 2019	$1,013.37	$280.67	$732.70	$195,105.15
Sep 2019	$1,013.37	$281.73	$731.64	$194,823.43
Oct 2019	$1,013.37	$282.78	$730.59	$194,540.65
Nov 2019	$1,013.37	$283.84	$729.53	$194,256.80
Dec 2019	$1,013.37	$284.91	$728.46	$193,971.89

Payment Date	Payment	Principal	Interest	Balance
Jan 2020	$1,013.37	$285.98	$727.39	$193,685.92
Feb 2020	$1,013.37	$287.05	$726.32	$193,398.87
Mar 2020	$1,013.37	$288.12	$725.25	$193,110.75
Apr 2020	$1,013.37	$289.21	$724.17	$192,821.54
May 2020	$1,013.37	$290.29	$723.08	$192,531.25
Jun 2020	$1,013.37	$291.38	$721.99	$192,239.87
Jul 2020	$1,013.37	$292.47	$720.90	$191,947.40
Aug 2020	$1,013.37	$293.57	$719.80	$191,653.83
Sep 2020	$1,013.37	$294.67	$718.70	$191,359.16
Oct 2020	$1,013.37	$295.77	$717.60	$191,063.39
Nov 2020	$1,013.37	$296.88	$716.49	$190,766.51
Dec 2020	$1,013.37	$298.00	$715.37	$190,468.51
Jan 2021	$1,013.37	$299.11	$714.26	$190,169.40
Feb 2021	$1,013.37	$300.24	$713.14	$189,869.16
Mar 2021	$1,013.37	$301.36	$712.01	$189,567.80
Apr 2021	$1,013.37	$302.49	$710.88	$189,265.31
May 2021	$1,013.37	$303.63	$709.74	$188,961.68
Jun 2021	$1,013.37	$304.76	$708.61	$188,656.92

Payment Date	Payment	Principal	Interest	Balance
Jul 2021	$1,013.37	$305.91	$707.46	$188,351.01
Aug 2021	$1,013.37	$307.05	$706.32	$188,043.96
Sep 2021	$1,013.37	$308.21	$705.16	$187,735.75
Oct 2021	$1,013.37	$309.36	$704.01	$187,426.39
Nov 2021	$1,013.37	$310.52	$702.85	$187,115.87
Dec 2021	$1,013.37	$311.69	$701.68	$186,804.18
Jan 2022	$1,013.37	$312.85	$700.52	$186,491.33
Feb 2022	$1,013.37	$314.03	$699.34	$186,177.30
Mar 2022	$1,013.37	$315.21	$698.16	$185,862.09
Apr 2022	$1,013.37	$316.39	$696.98	$185,545.71
May 2022	$1,013.37	$317.57	$695.80	$185,228.13
Jun 2022	$1,013.37	$318.77	$694.61	$184,909.37
Jul 2022	$1,013.37	$319.96	$693.41	$184,589.41
Aug 2022	$1,013.37	$321.16	$692.21	$184,268.25
Sep 2022	$1,013.37	$322.36	$691.01	$183,945.88
Oct 2022	$1,013.37	$323.57	$689.80	$183,622.31
Nov 2022	$1,013.37	$324.79	$688.58	$183,297.52
Dec 2022	$1,013.37	$326.00	$687.37	$182,971.52

Payment Date	Payment	Principal	Interest	Balance
Jan 2023	$1,013.37	$327.23	$686.14	$182,644.29
Feb 2023	$1,013.37	$328.45	$684.92	$182,315.83
Mar 2023	$1,013.37	$329.69	$683.68	$181,986.15
Apr 2023	$1,013.37	$330.92	$682.45	$181,655.23
May 2023	$1,013.37	$332.16	$681.21	$181,323.06
Jun 2023	$1,013.37	$333.41	$679.96	$180,989.65
Jul 2023	$1,013.37	$334.66	$678.71	$180,654.99
Aug 2023	$1,013.37	$335.91	$677.46	$180,319.08
Sep 2023	$1,013.37	$337.17	$676.20	$179,981.90
Oct 2023	$1,013.37	$338.44	$674.93	$179,643.47
Nov 2023	$1,013.37	$339.71	$673.66	$179,303.76
Dec 2023	$1,013.37	$340.98	$672.39	$178,962.78
Jan 2024	$1,013.37	$342.26	$671.11	$178,620.52
Feb 2024	$1,013.37	$343.54	$669.83	$178,276.97
Mar 2024	$1,013.37	$344.83	$668.54	$177,932.14
Apr 2024	$1,013.37	$346.13	$667.25	$177,586.02
May 2024	$1,013.37	$347.42	$665.95	$177,238.59
Jun 2024	$1,013.37	$348.73	$664.64	$176,889.87

Payment Date	Payment	Principal	Interest	Balance
Jul 2024	$1,013.37	$350.03	$663.34	$176,539.83
Aug 2024	$1,013.37	$351.35	$662.02	$176,188.49
Sep 2024	$1,013.37	$352.66	$660.71	$175,835.82
Oct 2024	$1,013.37	$353.99	$659.38	$175,481.84
Nov 2024	$1,013.37	$355.31	$658.06	$175,126.52
Dec 2024	$1,013.37	$356.65	$656.72	$174,769.88
Jan 2025	$1,013.37	$357.98	$655.39	$174,411.89
Feb 2025	$1,013.37	$359.33	$654.04	$174,052.57
Mar 2025	$1,013.37	$360.67	$652.70	$173,691.89
Apr 2025	$1,013.37	$362.03	$651.34	$173,329.87
May 2025	$1,013.37	$363.38	$649.99	$172,966.48
Jun 2025	$1,013.37	$364.75	$648.62	$172,601.74
Jul 2025	$1,013.37	$366.11	$647.26	$172,235.62
Aug 2025	$1,013.37	$367.49	$645.88	$171,868.14
Sep 2025	$1,013.37	$368.87	$644.51	$171,499.27
Oct 2025	$1,013.37	$370.25	$643.12	$171,129.02
Nov 2025	$1,013.37	$371.64	$641.73	$170,757.39
Dec 2025	$1,013.37	$373.03	$640.34	$170,384.36

Payment Date	Payment	Principal	Interest	Balance
Jan 2026	$1,013.37	$374.43	$638.94	$170,009.93
Feb 2026	$1,013.37	$375.83	$637.54	$169,634.09
Mar 2026	$1,013.37	$377.24	$636.13	$169,256.85
Apr 2026	$1,013.37	$378.66	$634.71	$168,878.19
May 2026	$1,013.37	$380.08	$633.29	$168,498.12
Jun 2026	$1,013.37	$381.50	$631.87	$168,116.61
Jul 2026	$1,013.37	$382.93	$630.44	$167,733.68
Aug 2026	$1,013.37	$384.37	$629.00	$167,349.31
Sep 2026	$1,013.37	$385.81	$627.56	$166,963.50
Oct 2026	$1,013.37	$387.26	$626.11	$166,576.24
Nov 2026	$1,013.37	$388.71	$624.66	$166,187.53
Dec 2026	$1,013.37	$390.17	$623.20	$165,797.37
Jan 2027	$1,013.37	$391.63	$621.74	$165,405.74
Feb 2027	$1,013.37	$393.10	$620.27	$165,012.64
Mar 2027	$1,013.37	$394.57	$618.80	$164,618.06
Apr 2027	$1,013.37	$396.05	$617.32	$164,222.01
May 2027	$1,013.37	$397.54	$615.83	$163,824.47
Jun 2027	$1,013.37	$399.03	$614.34	$163,425.44

Payment Date	Payment	Principal	Interest	Balance
Jul 2027	$1,013.37	$400.53	$612.85	$163,024.92
Aug 2027	$1,013.37	$402.03	$611.34	$162,622.89
Sep 2027	$1,013.37	$403.53	$609.84	$162,219.36
Oct 2027	$1,013.37	$405.05	$608.32	$161,814.31
Nov 2027	$1,013.37	$406.57	$606.80	$161,407.74
Dec 2027	$1,013.37	$408.09	$605.28	$160,999.65
Jan 2028	$1,013.37	$409.62	$603.75	$160,590.03
Feb 2028	$1,013.37	$411.16	$602.21	$160,178.87
Mar 2028	$1,013.37	$412.70	$600.67	$159,766.17
Apr 2028	$1,013.37	$414.25	$599.12	$159,351.92
May 2028	$1,013.37	$415.80	$597.57	$158,936.12
Jun 2028	$1,013.37	$417.36	$596.01	$158,518.76
Jul 2028	$1,013.37	$418.93	$594.45	$158,099.84
Aug 2028	$1,013.37	$420.50	$592.87	$157,679.34
Sep 2028	$1,013.37	$422.07	$591.30	$157,257.27
Oct 2028	$1,013.37	$423.66	$589.71	$156,833.61
Nov 2028	$1,013.37	$425.24	$588.13	$156,408.37
Dec 2028	$1,013.37	$426.84	$586.53	$155,981.53

Payment Date	Payment	Principal	Interest	Balance
Jan 2029	$1,013.37	$428.44	$584.93	$155,553.09
Feb 2029	$1,013.37	$430.05	$583.32	$155,123.04
Mar 2029	$1,013.37	$431.66	$581.71	$154,691.38
Apr 2029	$1,013.37	$433.28	$580.09	$154,258.10
May 2029	$1,013.37	$434.90	$578.47	$153,823.20
Jun 2029	$1,013.37	$436.53	$576.84	$153,386.67
Jul 2029	$1,013.37	$438.17	$575.20	$152,948.50
Aug 2029	$1,013.37	$439.81	$573.56	$152,508.68
Sep 2029	$1,013.37	$441.46	$571.91	$152,067.22
Oct 2029	$1,013.37	$443.12	$570.25	$151,624.10
Nov 2029	$1,013.37	$444.78	$568.59	$151,179.32
Dec 2029	$1,013.37	$446.45	$566.92	$150,732.87
Jan 2030	$1,013.37	$448.12	$565.25	$150,284.75
Feb 2030	$1,013.37	$449.80	$563.57	$149,834.95
Mar 2030	$1,013.37	$451.49	$561.88	$149,383.46
Apr 2030	$1,013.37	$453.18	$560.19	$148,930.28
May 2030	$1,013.37	$454.88	$558.49	$148,475.39
Jun 2030	$1,013.37	$456.59	$556.78	$148,018.81

Payment Date	Payment	Principal	Interest	Balance
Jul 2030	$1,013.37	$458.30	$555.07	$147,560.51
Aug 2030	$1,013.37	$460.02	$553.35	$147,100.49
Sep 2030	$1,013.37	$461.74	$551.63	$146,638.74
Oct 2030	$1,013.37	$463.48	$549.90	$146,175.27
Nov 2030	$1,013.37	$465.21	$548.16	$145,710.05
Dec 2030	$1,013.37	$466.96	$546.41	$145,243.10
Jan 2031	$1,013.37	$468.71	$544.66	$144,774.39
Feb 2031	$1,013.37	$470.47	$542.90	$144,303.92
Mar 2031	$1,013.37	$472.23	$541.14	$143,831.69
Apr 2031	$1,013.37	$474.00	$539.37	$143,357.69
May 2031	$1,013.37	$475.78	$537.59	$142,881.91
Jun 2031	$1,013.37	$477.56	$535.81	$142,404.34
Jul 2031	$1,013.37	$479.35	$534.02	$141,924.99
Aug 2031	$1,013.37	$481.15	$532.22	$141,443.84
Sep 2031	$1,013.37	$482.96	$530.41	$140,960.88
Oct 2031	$1,013.37	$484.77	$528.60	$140,476.12
Nov 2031	$1,013.37	$486.59	$526.79	$139,989.53
Dec 2031	$1,013.37	$488.41	$524.96	$139,501.12

Payment Date	Payment	Principal	Interest	Balance
Jan 2032	$1,013.37	$490.24	$523.13	$139,010.88
Feb 2032	$1,013.37	$492.08	$521.29	$138,518.80
Mar 2032	$1,013.37	$493.93	$519.45	$138,024.87
Apr 2032	$1,013.37	$495.78	$517.59	$137,529.10
May 2032	$1,013.37	$497.64	$515.73	$137,031.46
Jun 2032	$1,013.37	$499.50	$513.87	$136,531.96
Jul 2032	$1,013.37	$501.38	$511.99	$136,030.58
Aug 2032	$1,013.37	$503.26	$510.11	$135,527.33
Sep 2032	$1,013.37	$505.14	$508.23	$135,022.18
Oct 2032	$1,013.37	$507.04	$506.33	$134,515.14
Nov 2032	$1,013.37	$508.94	$504.43	$134,006.21
Dec 2032	$1,013.37	$510.85	$502.52	$133,495.36
Jan 2033	$1,013.37	$512.76	$500.61	$132,982.60
Feb 2033	$1,013.37	$514.69	$498.68	$132,467.91
Mar 2033	$1,013.37	$516.62	$496.75	$131,951.29
Apr 2033	$1,013.37	$518.55	$494.82	$131,432.74
May 2033	$1,013.37	$520.50	$492.87	$130,912.24
Jun 2033	$1,013.37	$522.45	$490.92	$130,389.79

Payment Date	Payment	Principal	Interest	Balance
Jul 2033	$1,013.37	$524.41	$488.96	$129,865.38
Aug 2033	$1,013.37	$526.38	$487.00	$129,339.01
Sep 2033	$1,013.37	$528.35	$485.02	$128,810.66
Oct 2033	$1,013.37	$530.33	$483.04	$128,280.33
Nov 2033	$1,013.37	$532.32	$481.05	$127,748.01
Dec 2033	$1,013.37	$534.32	$479.06	$127,213.69
Jan 2034	$1,013.37	$536.32	$477.05	$126,677.37
Feb 2034	$1,013.37	$538.33	$475.04	$126,139.04
Mar 2034	$1,013.37	$540.35	$473.02	$125,598.69
Apr 2034	$1,013.37	$542.38	$471.00	$125,056.32
May 2034	$1,013.37	$544.41	$468.96	$124,511.91
Jun 2034	$1,013.37	$546.45	$466.92	$123,965.46
Jul 2034	$1,013.37	$548.50	$464.87	$123,416.96
Aug 2034	$1,013.37	$550.56	$462.81	$122,866.40
Sep 2034	$1,013.37	$552.62	$460.75	$122,313.78
Oct 2034	$1,013.37	$554.69	$458.68	$121,759.09
Nov 2034	$1,013.37	$556.77	$456.60	$121,202.31
Dec 2034	$1,013.37	$558.86	$454.51	$120,643.45

Payment Date	Payment	Principal	Interest	Balance
Jan 2035	$1,013.37	$560.96	$452.41	$120,082.49
Feb 2035	$1,013.37	$563.06	$450.31	$119,519.43
Mar 2035	$1,013.37	$565.17	$448.20	$118,954.26
Apr 2035	$1,013.37	$567.29	$446.08	$118,386.97
May 2035	$1,013.37	$569.42	$443.95	$117,817.55
Jun 2035	$1,013.37	$571.55	$441.82	$117,245.99
Jul 2035	$1,013.37	$573.70	$439.67	$116,672.29
Aug 2035	$1,013.37	$575.85	$437.52	$116,096.44
Sep 2035	$1,013.37	$578.01	$435.36	$115,518.44
Oct 2035	$1,013.37	$580.18	$433.19	$114,938.26
Nov 2035	$1,013.37	$582.35	$431.02	$114,355.91
Dec 2035	$1,013.37	$584.54	$428.83	$113,771.37
Jan 2036	$1,013.37	$586.73	$426.64	$113,184.64
Feb 2036	$1,013.37	$588.93	$424.44	$112,595.71
Mar 2036	$1,013.37	$591.14	$422.23	$112,004.58
Apr 2036	$1,013.37	$593.35	$420.02	$111,411.22
May 2036	$1,013.37	$595.58	$417.79	$110,815.65
Jun 2036	$1,013.37	$597.81	$415.56	$110,217.83

Payment Date	Payment	Principal	Interest	Balance
Jul 2036	$1,013.37	$600.05	$413.32	$109,617.78
Aug 2036	$1,013.37	$602.30	$411.07	$109,015.48
Sep 2036	$1,013.37	$604.56	$408.81	$108,410.91
Oct 2036	$1,013.37	$606.83	$406.54	$107,804.08
Nov 2036	$1,013.37	$609.11	$404.27	$107,194.98
Dec 2036	$1,013.37	$611.39	$401.98	$106,583.59
Jan 2037	$1,013.37	$613.68	$399.69	$105,969.91
Feb 2037	$1,013.37	$615.98	$397.39	$105,353.92
Mar 2037	$1,013.37	$618.29	$395.08	$104,735.63
Apr 2037	$1,013.37	$620.61	$392.76	$104,115.02
May 2037	$1,013.37	$622.94	$390.43	$103,492.08
Jun 2037	$1,013.37	$625.28	$388.10	$102,866.80
Jul 2037	$1,013.37	$627.62	$385.75	$102,239.18
Aug 2037	$1,013.37	$629.97	$383.40	$101,609.21
Sep 2037	$1,013.37	$632.34	$381.03	$100,976.87
Oct 2037	$1,013.37	$634.71	$378.66	$100,342.17
Nov 2037	$1,013.37	$637.09	$376.28	$99,705.08
Dec 2037	$1,013.37	$639.48	$373.89	$99,065.60

Payment Date	Payment	Principal	Interest	Balance
Jan 2038	$1,013.37	$641.87	$371.50	$98,423.73
Feb 2038	$1,013.37	$644.28	$369.09	$97,779.45
Mar 2038	$1,013.37	$646.70	$366.67	$97,132.75
Apr 2038	$1,013.37	$649.12	$364.25	$96,483.63
May 2038	$1,013.37	$651.56	$361.81	$95,832.07
Jun 2038	$1,013.37	$654.00	$359.37	$95,178.07
Jul 2038	$1,013.37	$656.45	$356.92	$94,521.62
Aug 2038	$1,013.37	$658.91	$354.46	$93,862.70
Sep 2038	$1,013.37	$661.39	$351.99	$93,201.32
Oct 2038	$1,013.37	$663.87	$349.50	$92,537.45
Nov 2038	$1,013.37	$666.36	$347.02	$91,871.09
Dec 2038	$1,013.37	$668.85	$344.52	$91,202.24
Jan 2039	$1,013.37	$671.36	$342.01	$90,530.88
Feb 2039	$1,013.37	$673.88	$339.49	$89,857.00
Mar 2039	$1,013.37	$676.41	$336.96	$89,180.59
Apr 2039	$1,013.37	$678.94	$334.43	$88,501.65
May 2039	$1,013.37	$681.49	$331.88	$87,820.16
Jun 2039	$1,013.37	$684.05	$329.33	$87,136.11

Payment Date	Payment	Principal	Interest	Balance
Jul 2039	$1,013.37	$686.61	$326.76	$86,449.50
Aug 2039	$1,013.37	$689.18	$324.19	$85,760.32
Sep 2039	$1,013.37	$691.77	$321.60	$85,068.55
Oct 2039	$1,013.37	$694.36	$319.01	$84,374.19
Nov 2039	$1,013.37	$696.97	$316.40	$83,677.22
Dec 2039	$1,013.37	$699.58	$313.79	$82,977.64
Jan 2040	$1,013.37	$702.20	$311.17	$82,275.43
Feb 2040	$1,013.37	$704.84	$308.53	$81,570.59
Mar 2040	$1,013.37	$707.48	$305.89	$80,863.11
Apr 2040	$1,013.37	$710.13	$303.24	$80,152.98
May 2040	$1,013.37	$712.80	$300.57	$79,440.18
Jun 2040	$1,013.37	$715.47	$297.90	$78,724.71
Jul 2040	$1,013.37	$718.15	$295.22	$78,006.56
Aug 2040	$1,013.37	$720.85	$292.52	$77,285.71
Sep 2040	$1,013.37	$723.55	$289.82	$76,562.16
Oct 2040	$1,013.37	$726.26	$287.11	$75,835.90
Nov 2040	$1,013.37	$728.99	$284.38	$75,106.92
Dec 2040	$1,013.37	$731.72	$281.65	$74,375.20

Payment Date	Payment	Principal	Interest	Balance
Jan 2041	$1,013.37	$734.46	$278.91	$73,640.73
Feb 2041	$1,013.37	$737.22	$276.15	$72,903.52
Mar 2041	$1,013.37	$739.98	$273.39	$72,163.53
Apr 2041	$1,013.37	$742.76	$270.61	$71,420.78
May 2041	$1,013.37	$745.54	$267.83	$70,675.23
Jun 2041	$1,013.37	$748.34	$265.03	$69,926.89
Jul 2041	$1,013.37	$751.14	$262.23	$69,175.75
Aug 2041	$1,013.37	$753.96	$259.41	$68,421.79
Sep 2041	$1,013.37	$756.79	$256.58	$67,665.00
Oct 2041	$1,013.37	$759.63	$253.74	$66,905.37
Nov 2041	$1,013.37	$762.48	$250.90	$66,142.90
Dec 2041	$1,013.37	$765.33	$248.04	$65,377.56
Jan 2042	$1,013.37	$768.20	$245.17	$64,609.36
Feb 2042	$1,013.37	$771.09	$242.29	$63,838.27
Mar 2042	$1,013.37	$773.98	$239.39	$63,064.29
Apr 2042	$1,013.37	$776.88	$236.49	$62,287.41
May 2042	$1,013.37	$779.79	$233.58	$61,507.62
Jun 2042	$1,013.37	$782.72	$230.65	$60,724.91

Payment Date	Payment	Principal	Interest	Balance
Jul 2042	$1,013.37	$785.65	$227.72	$59,939.25
Aug 2042	$1,013.37	$788.60	$224.77	$59,150.65
Sep 2042	$1,013.37	$791.56	$221.81	$58,359.10
Oct 2042	$1,013.37	$794.52	$218.85	$57,564.57
Nov 2042	$1,013.37	$797.50	$215.87	$56,767.07
Dec 2042	$1,013.37	$800.49	$212.88	$55,966.58
Jan 2043	$1,013.37	$803.50	$209.87	$55,163.08
Feb 2043	$1,013.37	$806.51	$206.86	$54,356.57
Mar 2043	$1,013.37	$809.53	$203.84	$53,547.04
Apr 2043	$1,013.37	$812.57	$200.80	$52,734.47
May 2043	$1,013.37	$815.62	$197.75	$51,918.85
Jun 2043	$1,013.37	$818.67	$194.70	$51,100.18
Jul 2043	$1,013.37	$821.74	$191.63	$50,278.43
Aug 2043	$1,013.37	$824.83	$188.54	$49,453.61
Sep 2043	$1,013.37	$827.92	$185.45	$48,625.69
Oct 2043	$1,013.37	$831.02	$182.35	$47,794.66
Nov 2043	$1,013.37	$834.14	$179.23	$46,960.52
Dec 2043	$1,013.37	$837.27	$176.10	$46,123.25

MORTGAGE SMART

Payment Date	Payment	Principal	Interest	Balance
Jan 2044	$1,013.37	$840.41	$172.96	$45,282.85
Feb 2044	$1,013.37	$843.56	$169.81	$44,439.29
Mar 2044	$1,013.37	$846.72	$166.65	$43,592.56
Apr 2044	$1,013.37	$849.90	$163.47	$42,742.66
May 2044	$1,013.37	$853.09	$160.28	$41,889.58
Jun 2044	$1,013.37	$856.28	$157.09	$41,033.29
Jul 2044	$1,013.37	$859.50	$153.87	$40,173.80
Aug 2044	$1,013.37	$862.72	$150.65	$39,311.08
Sep 2044	$1,013.37	$865.95	$147.42	$38,445.12
Oct 2044	$1,013.37	$869.20	$144.17	$37,575.92
Nov 2044	$1,013.37	$872.46	$140.91	$36,703.46
Dec 2044	$1,013.37	$875.73	$137.64	$35,827.73
Jan 2045	$1,013.37	$879.02	$134.35	$34,948.71
Feb 2045	$1,013.37	$882.31	$131.06	$34,066.40
Mar 2045	$1,013.37	$885.62	$127.75	$33,180.78
Apr 2045	$1,013.37	$888.94	$124.43	$32,291.84
May 2045	$1,013.37	$892.28	$121.09	$31,399.56
Jun 2045	$1,013.37	$895.62	$117.75	$30,503.94

Payment Date	Payment	Principal	Interest	Balance
Jul 2045	$1,013.37	$898.98	$114.39	$29,604.96
Aug 2045	$1,013.37	$902.35	$111.02	$28,702.60
Sep 2045	$1,013.37	$905.74	$107.63	$27,796.87
Oct 2045	$1,013.37	$909.13	$104.24	$26,887.74
Nov 2045	$1,013.37	$912.54	$100.83	$25,975.19
Dec 2045	$1,013.37	$915.96	$97.41	$25,059.23
Jan 2046	$1,013.37	$919.40	$93.97	$24,139.83
Feb 2046	$1,013.37	$922.85	$90.52	$23,216.99
Mar 2046	$1,013.37	$926.31	$87.06	$22,290.68
Apr 2046	$1,013.37	$929.78	$83.59	$21,360.90
May 2046	$1,013.37	$933.27	$80.10	$20,427.63
Jun 2046	$1,013.37	$936.77	$76.60	$19,490.86
Jul 2046	$1,013.37	$940.28	$73.09	$18,550.58
Aug 2046	$1,013.37	$943.81	$69.56	$17,606.78
Sep 2046	$1,013.37	$947.35	$66.03	$16,659.43
Oct 2046	$1,013.37	$950.90	$62.47	$15,708.54
Nov 2046	$1,013.37	$954.46	$58.91	$14,754.07
Dec 2046	$1,013.37	$958.04	$55.33	$13,796.03

Payment Date	Payment	Principal	Interest	Balance
Jan 2047	$1,013.37	$961.64	$51.74	$12,834.39
Feb 2047	$1,013.37	$965.24	$48.13	$11,869.15
Mar 2047	$1,013.37	$968.86	$44.51	$10,900.29
Apr 2047	$1,013.37	$972.49	$40.88	$9,927.80
May 2047	$1,013.37	$976.14	$37.23	$8,951.65
Jun 2047	$1,013.37	$979.80	$33.57	$7,971.85
Jul 2047	$1,013.37	$983.48	$29.89	$6,988.38
Aug 2047	$1,013.37	$987.16	$26.21	$6,001.21
Sep 2047	$1,013.37	$990.87	$22.50	$5,010.35
Oct 2047	$1,013.37	$994.58	$18.79	$4,015.76
Nov 2047	$1,013.37	$998.31	$15.06	$3,017.45
Dec 2047	$1,013.37	$1,002.06	$11.32	$2,015.40
Jan 2048	$1,013.37	$1,005.81	$7.56	$1,009.58
Feb 2048	$1,013.37	$1,009.58	$3.79	$0.00

As you can see, for each of the 360 payments due, there is a breakdown of what happens with that payment amount and what effect it has on the remainder of your loan. Note that this only addresses the repayment of the debt – the principal and interest

– and has nothing to do with your taxes, insurance, mortgage insurance or homeowner's association dues. (The exception would be if anything was added to your mortgage amount and had to be repaid, such as FHA upfront MIP.)

The amortization schedule can be used for more than just keeping track on where you are in the process of paying off your mortgage, as you will see in the next section.

25

PRE-PAYING PRINCIPAL TO REDUCE INTEREST CHARGES

Pre-paying some part of your principal before it is due can save you a lot of money in the long run. Assuming that there is no pre-payment penalty on your loan, you can make use of your amortization schedule to see what kind of effect pre-paying principal can have on your overall interest expense, and on when your loan will be paid in full.

For example, using the amortization schedule in the previous section, let's say that you purchased a home in January of 2018 and that your first monthly payment is due March 1st, 2018.

Referring to that first payment line in the amortization schedule, you will see that your payment amount is $1,013.37 per month. Of that amount, $750 will go to interest, leaving $263.37 to reduce your principal balance. After subtracting the principal payment from the original $200,000 loan amount, you will now owe $199,736.63 on your mortgage.

(In case you are curious, that $750 interest payment is your annual interest rate of 4.5% divided by 12 months, multiplied by the loan amount. A very simple calculation.)

The second month, you no longer owe the full $200,000 because you have made a small payment toward principal with your first payment. Therefore, your interest charge decreases slightly, leaving a little more of that monthly payment to go toward principal.

This is why at the beginning of your mortgage most of your payment goes toward interest, and toward the end of your mortgage most of your payment goes toward principal – you simply owe less money to pay interest on after you have spent years paying down your principal balance.

Here is where things get interesting. Let's say that on March 1st, 2018, at the same time you make your first mortgage payment of $1,013.37, you were also to make a principal-reduction payment of $264.36. By doing that, you just saved $749.01 in interest charges and advanced your payoff by one month.

Now, instead of having completed only the first line on your amortization schedule, you have completed the first two lines on the schedule. And, instead of owing another 359 payments (of the 360 total), you only owe 358 more payments.

At any time during your mortgage payoff process, you can look at the far right column of the amortization schedule and identify the line showing the balance number closest to your actual principal balance showed. This will be the line that shows you where you are in your mortgage payoff process, and how many payments you have left.

For example, let's say that you have been making payments for one year and you just received a bonus of $10,000 from your job. You decide that, instead of buying something nice or going on a trip, you would like to apply your bonus to paying down your mortgage balance.

At the end of one year, you have made 12 payments so you are now looking at payment #13 which is March 2019. After you have made the March 2019 payment, your principal balance due will be $196,498.08. In addition to that payment, you make a separate principal-reduction payment of $10,000. Now, instead of $196,498.08, you actually owe $186,498.08.

Next, you look for that number (or the closest number to that number that you can find) in the far right column. That number is $186,491.33. To find that number, you have to go all the way down to the January 2022 payment. This means that by making that extra $10,000 payment, you just advanced your payoff by skipping ahead 34 monthly payments! You have taken almost 3 years off of your repayment schedule and saved about $24,454.58 (34 payments of $1,013.37, less the $10,000 you paid to do that).

Looking at your amortization schedule can increase your motivation to pre-pay principal because you can see the huge effect this can have on your long-term financial situation. I suggest keeping a copy of your amortization schedule where you can access it quickly and easily. That way, when you are tempted to spend a sizable chunk of money on something that won't last, you can compare that expenditure with the benefits of putting that money toward paying down your mortgage.

It is useful to know that the effect of pre-paying principal seems to decrease the further you are in the payoff process. Pre-paying $10,000 of principal toward the end of your mortgage will not advance you on the amortization schedule as much as it will toward the beginning of your mortgage. This is because at the beginning of your mortgage your principal balance is higher so more interest is being accrued that can be saved by this pre-payment. If you compare the first payment to the last, this is easy to see:

Payment Date	Payment	Principal	Interest	Balance
Mar 2018	$1,013.37	$263.37	$750.00	$199,736.63
Feb 2048	$1,013.37	$1,009.58	$3.79	$0.00

Your first payment includes interest charges of $750, whereas your last payment only includes interest charges of $3.79. This is because at the time of your first payment you owe $200,000 and when you make your last payment you only owe $1009.58 (see Balance column from next-to-last payment).

Toward the end of your mortgage, the bigger benefit in pre-paying principal is simply that you are no longer in debt for that amount of money. This is also an important benefit and is often overlooked, as it seems to be overshadowed by a natural and healthy aversion to paying interest.

26

WHAT IS A RECAST?

A *recast* is a nice little secret that you may not be aware of. Allow me to explain this with an example.

Let's say that you owe $300,000 on your mortgage. You have come into a large sum of money, let's say $150,000, through an inheritance or by some other means. You would like to pre-pay some principal on your mortgage so that you only owe $150,000 instead of $300,000. There is no pre-payment penalty, so doing this is not a problem.

The only snag is that when you pre-pay principal to reduce your mortgage balance, this advances you on your amortization schedule so that your mortgage will be paid in full sooner than it was scheduled to. That's great – but it does not reduce your monthly payment amount.

In the long run, you will save more in interest charges if you keep making the same payment and allow this pre-payment to reduce the term of your loan. But, that might not be your need or your priority at the time. Maybe a change in employment or family status has made your current payment amount uncomfortable, so that you would really like to do something to bring that payment amount down.

This is what a recast does. With a recast, you do not have to refinance to change your monthly payment amount. Instead of changing the term and leaving your monthly payment as is, a recast allows you to leave the term where it is and change your monthly payment.

There are situations all the time where someone has a large chunk of money, but really needs to reduce their monthly obligations. A recast will do this – and much less expensively than a refinance.

That said, if mortgage rates have gone down, or maybe you need to get out from under an adjustable rate and move to a fixed rate, or for any number of other reasons, a refinance might be a great idea for you. But if the only thing you want to do is reduce your monthly payment amount by paying a big chunk of money toward your mortgage, a recast is probably the way to go.

To do a recast, you would contact the servicer of your

loan and ask about their procedure and what it costs. They might charge $250 or so – far less than a refinance. And they may allow only one during the loan period – or maybe one per year. This would be a very good question to ask them.

In my business as a mortgage loan officer, I have come across people who want to buy a house with a relatively small down payment and a 30-year term. They know they have a big chunk of money coming in at some point in the not-too-distant future. Their priority is to reduce their payment amount, not the term. They get their mortgage, wait their 6 months, or whatever the servicer requires, and do a recast. Mission accomplished.

You may or may not ever want to do a recast – but it is good to know that such an option exists.

27

REVERSE MORTGAGES, HELOC'S, LAND LOANS, CONSRUCTION LOANS, RENOVATION LOANS, SUBDIVISION SALES

There are many loan products, programs and options out there that I will not attempt to cover in this book. But it is good to at least have some idea of what some of these things are.

Reverse Mortgage:

A typical mortgage allows you to pay into your home, so to speak, for a large number of years then have that home paid off. So, what happens if, once you get that home paid off (or are fairly close) and you want to stay in the home, but your income was reduced by retirement, a health or family situation, etc.?

For some seniors, moving may be the right choice.

Something smaller, less expensive, more geared towards a senior lifestyle, etc. These can be good options. But what if you really, really want to stay in the home you have loved for years – but you just don't have the income to do that, even though the home itself is paid off?

Well, that home you took care of, by paying into it for all those years, can now take care of you by providing you with a monthly income to help you with your living expenses – instead of your having to make payments on the home. The equity you built up, through the repayment of the mortgage debt and appreciation in the real estate market, can now be given back to you to help you with other expenses.

Of course, this means that you will have an increasing debt secured by your home. But, this debt will not require a monthly payment. So, the issue here is cash flow. It may be that your kids are just fine, financially. Maybe they don't need to inherit your house nearly as much as you need the cash flow from being able to access your home equity to help with your monthly financial obligations.

If this is the case, then a reverse mortgage might be right for you. This debt will accrue interest during the time that you owe money, but that interest will not be due until your death or some other trigger such as selling or moving out of the home. You can continue to live off this debt until you float off into the sunset, at which time your house will be sold to repay the debt. Any residual equity will be distributed to your heirs.

I do not recommend this to everyone. But if your situation fits what this product was designed for, it may be a good option. I suggest going over your options with an honest, objective financial advisor and evaluating those options carefully to determine if this is right for you.

HELOC:

A HELOC is a ***H****ome **E**quity **L**ine **O**f Credit*. This is an *open-end* debt secured by your home. That means it is revolving – you have a credit limit and can access part or all of that limit whenever you like. You can pay back part or all of that limit, then access it again later.

Since a HELOC allows you to borrow money later – and interest rates change over time – a HELOC uses a variable interest rate, like a credit card or any other open-end loan.

These lines of credit can be used as a type of *second mortgage* (a mortgage with foreclosure for recovery rights that are second in line to your first, or primary, mortgage). They can also be used as the only debt instrument secured by your home.

If you own your house outright and decide that you would like to borrow against your house for some reason, you can look at what you need the money for, then decide if a *closed-end* loan (installment loan, regular mortgage) or an open-end loan would be more suitable.

If you want to make a one-time expenditure very soon and simply make a regular monthly payment over time to repay that loan, maybe a **cash-out refinance** is the way to go (refinancing your home to pull cash out of your equity).

But, if you need ongoing access to funds and want to be able to repay money and borrow it again without paying interest when you are not using the money – that sounds more like an open-ended, line of credit, or HELOC.

Some HELOC's may allow you to access part of your total available line of credit in the form of an installment loan at a fixed rate. This option would convert that partial amount to a closed-end loan with a fixed monthly payment, and leave the remainder as revolving debt that you can use and pay back as you wish.

Again, check this out in more detail to understand your options better. If you are interested in a HELOC, your lender can fill you in on what you need to know. It is a good option for the right situation.

Land Loan:

If you just want to buy a piece of land, maybe a building lot to build your own home on afterwards, this is a different type of loan than a regular mortgage. Many mortgage companies do not offer land loans, as they are riskier to the lender. If you decide on a land loan, you might have to ask around to find a good contact at the right financial institution.

If you are interested in a land loan, be prepared to put down a higher percentage of the purchase price than if you are buying an existing home. Also be prepared for higher interest rates.

For the right person and situation, a land loan is a perfect match. Just realize that it is a different type of loan.

Construction Loan:

This is also a different kind of loan than when you buy an existing house. A construction loan will allow you to be approved for a certain amount of money, then the lender will release this amount in installments based on the phase of construction as the project progresses. These types of loans have more moving parts, so to speak, than a regular loan does, so expect that to affect fees and interest rates.

Construction loans are designed to be temporary. When construction on your home has completed and all the money has been distributed, it will be time to take out ***permanent financing***. This means you get a "regular" mortgage which will pay off the construction loan. Now, you just have a regular house payment like everybody else.

There does exist a type of loan they might call ***construction-to-perm***, or something similar, which starts out as a construction loan then, when construction is complete, converts to permanent financing. Some lenders offer this type of loan and others to not. Many mortgage lenders do not offer construction loans, but enough do that you will be able to find one if that is what you are looking for.

Renovation Loan:

This is another specialized product. A renovation loan, or **reno** loan, is designed to allow you to borrow more than you are actually paying for the house itself.

This is because, as part of your home purchase, you intend to make certain improvements that have been planned, evaluated and approved in advance. This loan will set aside funds to make these improvements so that you can buy the home and fix it up all in the same loan. Again, there are additional "moving parts" with this kind of loan, so expect that to be considered in your rates and fees.

Subdivision Sales:

I don't think I can explain this adequately without offending someone – so, here I go again.

My first career right out of college was in subdivision sales, so I have been on that side of the desk. Somewhere along the line, subdivision builders decided that it is in their best interest to control who the lender is when a buyer is purchasing one of their homes. There are a variety of reasons for this, some less objectionable than others.

The fact is that, when you go to buy a new home from a subdivision builder, they are putting their money on the line – or their credit, and probably both. They are taking care of the financing during the construction phase of your home so that you will not need to obtain a construction loan. You only need to close on a traditional mortgage when the home is ready to move into.

The builder needs to know that a pre-approval letter really means that you are going to be able to buy their home. Otherwise, they could be left trying to sell a home that was what *you* wanted – but maybe not exactly what someone else will want.

There have been some lenders in the past (and probably present) that have issued pre-approval letters that may not accurately assess the buyer's ability to actually close on a loan. Some builders will not even accept pre-approval letters from lenders with this reputation, or they will at least require that you have been pre-approved by their preferred lender as well.

In addition to this valid reason to have some level of control over the lending process, there is another reason which may not be viewed as quite as legitimate.

Builders have discovered that if they own a mortgage company, in addition to construction and land development companies, their potential earnings and profits increase substantially. It is nice to offer in-house alternatives to their homebuyers, especially when there is some specific advantage to the buyer to keeping the entire process under one roof.

But, in the past, builders have tried to abuse this idea by requiring that their buyers use their mortgage company to finance their home purchase. And when they are able to control who the lender is, suddenly their mortgage company doesn't have offer terms that are very competitive with other mortgage companies. I have seen it with my own eyes – and it's not pretty.

Some ruling, law or regulation now prohibits builders from requiring that their buyers use their mortgage company. Yippie!! Well, not so fast. Subdivision builders quickly made an adjustment to the strategy that has a similar effect.

Not always – but in general, builders now mark up the price of their homes to allow room to offer some type of incentive to their buyers. But, this incentive is only given to buyers who agree to use the builder's "preferred lender". They're willing to give you your own money back – if you will give them even more money. How sneaky.

This incentive may be some allowance at the design center (where the markups are huge, so they're really not giving away as much as it looks like). Or, it may be paying for the title policy and some credit toward closing costs. Either way, most subdivision builders really, really want you to use their lender. And with most of the big builders, they own that lender.

Right now, this very month, I have a borrower who is going to close on a new home in one of these subdivisions. I was able to beat that builder's lender – including all the incentives being offered to use that lender. This is very often not the case. In this particular case, the builder does not own the lender, so the incentive was not as large as I have sometimes seen it.

In many cases, the incentive is so big that they are, in effect, forcing you to use their lender. This will probably be the case more often when the builder owns the lender and stands to make a larger profit from this customer if they can get both the home sale and the mortgage.

Just remember that these incentives are added to the price you are paying for the home. Also remember that everything is negotiable. If you don't want to use that builder's lender, tell them you are willing to buy the home, but only if they will include the incentive even though you will be using your own lender. They can accept that offer or refuse it, usually depending upon what the market looks like.

Also keep in mind that if the builder is simply offering to pay for the title policy if you use their lender, it is pretty standard among resale homes for the seller to pay for the title policy. I have a hard time looking at this as an incentive, so I would ask for this anyway.

It is good to keep in mind that the builder does have the right to have a pretty good idea that you will, in fact, be able to obtain the financing necessary to close on the home. But, I think when they brow-beat you into using their lender against your will, that's going too far.

I remember being in a meeting where the division president was yelling at us rather violently for not having a high enough percentage of our sales going through the builder-owned mortgage company (maybe because they had no local office and were really not that good). I was at 75% – three out of four of my home buyers were using our mortgage company. Not good enough.

Someone in the room dared to ask what would happen if we were not able to convince more buyers to use our mortgage company. The president's response actually shocked me. He said, "It's going to get to a point where if they won't use (name deleted) Mortgage, they can't buy the house!" True story. Not only is that unbelievably stupid (no offense), it's also not legal.

I would like to add one more comment about subdivision builders. In almost every case, the builder will pay for you to use a Realtor to represent you. I would like to suggest, most emphatically, that you take advantage of this.

Builder contracts are not the state-promulgated forms. They are written by the builder's attorneys. In my observation, these contracts are ALWAYS written to favor the builder over the buyer.

I have seen a lot of things that should have happened differently – I won't go into detail here. Just trust me on this and get professional representation. The builder has already priced this expense into the home. Take advantage of it and take a good Realtor with you when you are house shopping at new subdivisions.

28

CONCLUSION – WHAT? ALREADY?

There are many loan products, programs and options out there that I will not attempt to cover in this book. I also left out a lot of detail that I thought was unnecessary for our purposes here. The purpose of this book is not to train loan officers, turn you into a loan officer, or to try to render loan officers unnecessary (which would, at best, be an exercise in futility).

It is important, however, to be able to understand your mortgage options, make the best choices for your individual situation, and know what is going on during the loan process.

If you are new to the financing of residential real estate, I am quite confident that you have learned something from this book. I'm also confident that you will have additional questions as you go through the mortgage process.

There is a lot more to know and I am sure that you will continue to learn as you go through your own mortgage experiences. I sincerely hope that reading this book has helped prepare you to be "mortgage smart" as you get started with or continue to go through the mortgage process.

Rico Wilson, CFP®

If you are interested in purchasing a home for yourself or your family – or if you are interested in residential property as an investment, please feel free to contact me personally.

I originate mortgages for properties located in Texas. If you need a mortgage in a different state, I would be happy to locate a good loan officer for you in that state.

Rico Wilson
512-633-7953 (My personal cell phone)
www.RicoWilson.com (website)
www.RicoMortgage.com (online loan application)
RicoMortgageBanker@gmail.com (personal email)

ABOUT THE AUTHOR

Rico Wilson has had many years of education, training and experience in Finance and Real Estate, which have prepared him well to work in the field of Mortgage Banking. In addition to his financial certifications, Rico has also earned numerous certifications in various therapeutic modalities that deal with subconscious reprogramming.

He has authored a number of books and classes on personal finance, real estate investing, and personal growth & development; and is also an accomplished musician/singer/songwriter. Most importantly, Rico is very happy to be a husband, father and grandfather to a wonderful wife, daughter, son-in-law and five awesome grandkids.

Rico and his wife, Valerie, live in Austin, Texas. When not at work or working on a project like this, Rico & Valerie enjoy dining out, travel, movies, music and frequent urban hikes in the sunshine.

Other Books & Classes by Rico Wilson

No Problem!
(The Solution to Pretty Much Everything)

Released in February, 2018, this new book contains the solution to just about every problem you will ever come across. When you program your subconscious mind with *Rico's Presuppositions Re: Problems & Solutions*, your mind will automatically deal with "problems" in a new way, helping you to turn everything to your advantage. Once you experience the difference, you will never want to go back.

Seven Weeks to a Positive Life

This book will help you to improve every aspect of your life by developing seven key mental habits. These habits will increase your level of happiness and satisfaction, reduce stress and frustration, change your reactions to events and circumstances and, ultimately, improve the circumstances that contribute to your overall life experience. (Standard or Large-Print)

Program Your Mind for Massive Success

This 3-hour course will teach you how your initial subconscious programming happened and how you can change it. It also demonstrates how this programming affects your life and your business. This live class is the pre-requisite to the more advanced class listed below.

Creating Miracles in Life & Business

This 2-day, 10-hour, live class is a continuation of *Program Your Mind for Massive Success*. It teaches a number of unique concepts and techniques that can help you to change your subconscious programming, release any negative emotions and completely transform your life and business. Some of this information is proprietary and can presently not be found anywhere else.

The Money Game

This game comes in the form of a workbook, and is a simplified, accelerated financial simulation that will allow you to experience, in fast-forward, the long-term effects of making certain financial decisions. The results you get from this game will become leading indicators for your real life and will help you to produce the results that you desire for your reality.

Success for Losers

Rico's first book on the subject of subconscious programming, *Success for Losers* is a great introduction to how your mind may have been programmed with some information that could be limiting your results and satisfaction in life. Of course, this book can also help you to improve that programming.

The Rico Strategy®

The strategy taught in this book represents an innovation in how real estate investors can earn money from investing in properties. *The Rico Strategy®* unveils a new source of profit that had previously gone unnoticed. This instructional textbook provides clear and thorough training on how to utilize this innovative strategy.

Trading Debt for Wealth

This workbook teaches the financial lay person how money, debt and compound interest can work for or against them. Rico's proprietary formula helps to prioritize debt acceleration and the workbook helps the student to get a much better grasp on how to manage their personal finances.

www.ingramcontent.com/pod-product-compliance
Lightning Source LLC
Chambersburg PA
CBHW071053240526
45471CB00015B/1785